Introducing
Reader's Workshop

Supporting Our Youngest Readers

Authors

Patricia Dade and Kimberly Storey

SHELL EDUCATION

Publishing Credits

Dona Herweck Rice, *Editor-in-Chief*; Lee Aucoin, *Creative Director*;
Don Tran, *Print Production Manager;* Conni Medina, M.A.Ed., *Editorial Director*;
Sara Johnson, *Senior Editor;* Hillary Wolfe, *Editor;*
Juan Chavolla, *Cover Artist/Interior Layout;* Corinne Burton, M.S.Ed., *Publisher*

Shell Education
5301 Oceanus Drive
Huntington Beach, CA 92649-1030
http://www.shelleducation.com
ISBN 978-1-4258-0702-3
©2011 Shell Educational Publishing, Inc.

Table of Contents

Table of Contents *(cont.)*

Introduction and Research

Sometimes, the hardest changes reap the most benefits. When the Blue Springs Missouri School District asked its teachers to completely change the way they taught reading, we realized that meant no more basal readers, worksheets, pre-generated questions, and basic recall. The new initiative was called Reader's Workshop. This approach involved long periods of independent reading time, scholarly discussion between students and teachers, and students who read books of their choosing at appropriate levels. In order to make their teachers as successful as possible, Blue Springs brought in several trailblazers and masters of reading instruction. Throughout the next several years, teachers worked with Ellin Keene, Debbie Miller, and Laura Robb to begin transforming their classrooms, teaching styles, and their own thinking to help students flourish.

As literacy coaches, our job was to aid the teachers in this process. Even though, between the two of us, we have over 40 years of teaching experience, we were the students in this area. It became our job to learn as much as we could about the Reader's Workshop process and pass that knowledge on to our colleagues. We practiced team teaching, modeled lessons, and provided a sounding board for our teachers' concerns, questions, and successes. While we certainly did not have all the answers, through collaboration and teamwork, we (along with our teachers) experienced many triumphs.

Reader's Workshop quickly took off in grades 3–5. Almost immediately, we detected a change in our students, teachers, and school as a whole. A casual observer would have immediately noticed that desks were often abandoned for more comfortable Reading Zones. Harsh overhead lights were turned off and replaced by the soft glow of lamps. Classrooms became intimate and inviting. But most significantly, students became engaged in their reading in a way the teachers had never seen before. The teachers were no longer solely responsible for the instruction in the classroom. Students began teaching students, discussions became more respectful and sophisticated, and more importantly, students began to rediscover the pure joy of reading.

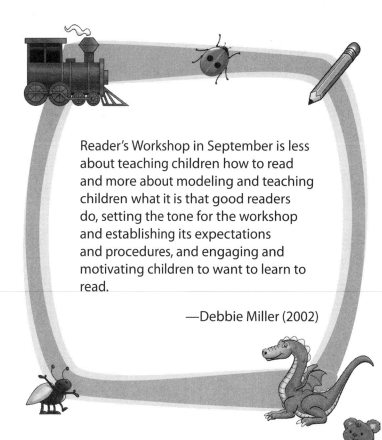

Reader's Workshop in September is less about teaching children how to read and more about modeling and teaching children what it is that good readers do, setting the tone for the workshop and establishing its expectations and procedures, and engaging and motivating children to want to learn to read.

—Debbie Miller (2002)

Introduction and Research *(cont.)*

In the primary grades, we saw many successes in student thinking. Teacher concern that high-level comprehension was too advanced for such young minds was quickly replaced by astonishment and delight at what their students understood. However, the teachers at the primary level had a more problematic task than the upper grades. As literacy coaches, we began to notice that most of the concerns brought to us were not about the components, but how to develop the underlying rituals and routines of the Reader's Workshop model and increase stamina during reading time. Again and again we heard comments, such as:

★ "How do I get students ready for Reader's Workshop when some of them have no book experience and most can't read?"

★ "What specifically are the procedures and routines needed to create a Reader's Workshop that runs smoothly and effectively? How do I get there?"

★ "How does everyone stay on task and engaged during independent reading? My students have never read for 30 minutes! How do I do that?"

As more teachers came to us with these types of questions, we realized we needed to focus on the routines and structures that would make future learning possible. This would be vital to the success of Reader's Workshop in the primary grades. And so, the process of planning for the success of our youngest readers began.

—Patricia and Kim

Introduction and Research (cont.)

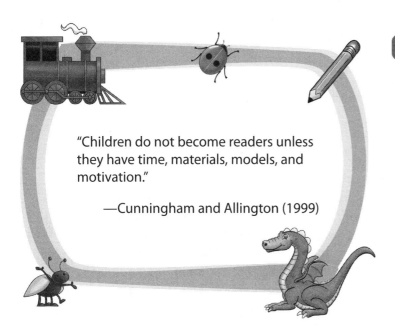

"Children do not become readers unless they have time, materials, models, and motivation."

—Cunningham and Allington (1999)

Think-Alouds

How can a teacher expect primary students to use higher-level thinking skills, read for extended periods of time, and make appropriate book choices? Research is clear: modeling, modeling, modeling. Teacher think-alouds provide a time to explicitly teach students strategies and skills to improve their reading. "The explicitness with which teachers teach…makes a difference in learner outcomes, especially for students who are low achieving and who profit from greater explicitness" (Block, Gambrell, and Pressley 2002).

Modeling reading behaviors through think-alouds assists in the Reader's Workshop process by setting a tone of calm, thoughtful learning in a literate environment. It also guides students in their own independent work and builds confidence in early readers (Miller 2002). Teacher think-alouds also allow students to hear the language of literature. Hearing books read aloud permits children to become familiar with the structures, language, patterns, and the relationships between books and the reader (Dorn and Soffos 2005).

Independent Reading Time

Reading is more than just word calling. Without comprehension, students miss the most important aspect of reading. In order for students to become efficient readers and to have deep comprehension of text, they need time to independently practice strategies modeled by other students and teachers. The correlation between reading achievement and time spent reading in the classroom is clear. The most significant improvements have been found when students are reading thoughtful and connected text, as opposed to simple sentences or isolated words (Block, Gambrell, and Pressley 2002).

Besides allowing students time to practice reading strategies, independent reading time can be a time when students "orchestrate all they know about reading…" (Calkins 2001). According to Collins (2004), independent reading time allows readers to:

★ have time to read and select "just-right" books
★ learn to take care of books
★ respect each other's reading time and reading lives
★ have daily opportunities for genuine talk about their reading
★ read the words and understand the story
★ work in an independent reading workshop that is replicable outside of the classroom

Introduction and Research *(cont.)*

Book Choices

Motivation to read is vital when creating an environment where students can work independently for extended periods of time. Evidence suggests, in order to have proficient comprehension of text, students not only need to have the skills, but also the desire to read. Motivation and achievement have been directly linked—the more students read, the more they learn about the world and can make connections to future reading. So how do we motivate students to read? One way is to provide students with texts that interest them (Block, Gambrell, and Pressley 2002). Engagement increases when students read books that link to their own lives, or are provided a choice in what they read. As engagement increases, so do comprehension, motivation, and fluency. Simply put, "When immersed in compelling text and equipped with comprehension strategies, children will reach further, probe deeper, and understand complex material from the earliest ages" (Keene and Zimmerman 2007).

Conferring

Independent reading time allows teachers to work one-on-one with students, a model of instruction that is very difficult to accomplish in a primary classroom. This conferring time allows teachers the opportunity to work with students and to reach each child's individual needs. Only in individual conferences are teachers able to specifically identify the needs of a student, thus assisting the student in becoming more independent in his or her reading skills (Keene and Zimmerman 2007).

Conferring also provides the teacher with an opportunity to assist each student in creating his or her own individual reading goal. These individual conferences allow the teacher to meet the students' needs, guiding them in finding goals in their own reading that will extend their thinking into more meaningful understanding. It is true that effective, direct instruction assists students in building comprehension. However, direct instruction can be more easily applied when teacher and student collaborate to extend understanding (Block, Gambrell, and Pressley 2002).

Getting Ready

Room Arrangement

Room arrangement is a big part of building a successful Reader's Workshop. At the beginning of the school year, even before the students arrive, teachers are busy putting together, decorating, and sprucing up their rooms. The same attention applies when creating a Reader's Workshop classroom. As teachers, we have to make explicit plans and reorganize our traditional classroom furnishings to include four key areas:

A Large Group Meeting Spot

- ★ A Large Group Meeting Spot
- ★ A Small Group Meeting Spot
- ★ Reading Zones
- ★ An accessible classroom library

Large Group Meeting Spot

This is a place where the entire class can sit together on the floor, generally with an easel or board for charts, often designated with an area rug. After independent reading, students return to the Large Group Meeting Spot to reflect, forming an oval around the teacher so they can respond to each other.

A Small Group Meeting Spot

Small Group Meeting Spot

This is where four to six students work with the teacher in invitational groups, book clubs, and collaborative projects. A round or kidney-shaped table with chairs works well. If space is limited, use stools that store under the table instead of chairs.

Reading Zones

These are spaces around the room where students read independently or with buddies. Use a combination of floor areas, cozy book nooks, and work spaces. Allow enough space in your classroom so students can work away from their desks if they choose. Classroom sizes vary, so expect students to be reading in close proximity to each other.

A Reading Zone

During independent reading time, students can choose or be assigned to a designated Reading Zone.

Getting Ready (cont.)

Classroom library with leveled basket labels

Classroom library with books by genre

Classroom Library

Making a book selection is hard work for many young readers, but finding books in an unorganized library can be overwhelming.

Classroom libraries can no longer consist of shelves lined with books—they must have a deliberate design. At the beginning of the year, allow time for students to become familiar with the books in the classroom. Have students help identify books that are similar or seem to go together. Guide learners toward key categories by limiting the quantity and type during book sorting sessions.

One kindergarten teacher started her sorting process by presenting her students with a large container of books. This represented only a small portion of her classroom library collection. The container was filled with thoughtfully selected books reflecting clear, predetermined categories. Using this method, students were not overwhelmed, but were instead empowered to make knowledgeable decisions. She continued this process over the next several days until no obvious groupings remained. Following these carefully planned sessions, students were ready to sort the remaining books. Final categories were solely student generated, as long as they could justify their thinking. This teacher's goal was for the students to have complete ownership of their classroom library. (Lessons that mirror this process are provided in this book.)

Categories might be as straightforward as favorite character series. Or, create more elaborate categories, separating books by author, standard genre, and reading level. Any category is acceptable, as long as students can defend their thinking for the connecting theme. In one classroom, they was even a category called, "Animals Who Wear Clothes." This nonstandard classification was definitely not what the teacher had in mind, but her students provided the necessary justification behind their decision, so it stayed. If organizing books by reading levels, be sure that no more than one-third of a classroom library is leveled.

Atmosphere

Reader's Workshop in action

"Creating environments that nurture literacy and foster independence requires thoughtful planning."

—Debbie Miller (2002)

Use unique lighting

When you read a book at home, which do you prefer—sitting at the kitchen table under bright lights, or curling up in a comfortable chair with soft light filtering across the room? This is an easy choice for most of us and it is the same with children!

Now that you have arranged and decorated your classroom, does it reflect an attitude that will be supportive of your students in this new reading model? A Reader's Workshop classroom environment sets the tone that allows your students to open up and be drawn into the comfortable folds of literature. It must be a place to take risks, experiment, and share.

Begin adding a little ambiance to your room with some of these suggestions:

Other lighting options

Incorporate Lamp Lighting

Lamps provide warm, natural lighting and a tranquil feel to the classroom. Teachers have used a wide variety of fixtures: hanging lanterns, chandeliers, torch and octopus floor lamps, table lamps, and even holiday lights.

Getting Ready *(cont.)*

Classroom Library *(cont.)*

As categories are identified, place books in baskets or bins and have children label each one. Utilizing baskets allows students to flip through books easily and labeled categories help them locate desired books quickly. Involving students in this organizational process gives them a sense of ownership of the classroom library. Students will be more apt to return books to their proper places because they determined where the books belonged.

When setting up your classroom library, think about ways your categories can support differentiated instruction. Books are categorized to make sense to young learners and their ways of thinking. An example of some ways to organize categories to accommodate different learning styles is shown at right.

Classroom Library Catego[ries] Support Differentiation

Kindergarten and First Grad[e] Standard Genres
- ★ nonfiction
- ★ song books
- ★ alphabet books
- ★ number books
- ★ fairy tales
- ★ people books
- ★ animal books
- ★ character sets
- ★ award-winning books

Second Grade Standard Genr[es]
- ★ classic/traditional
- ★ realistic fiction
- ★ historical fiction
- ★ fantasy
- ★ mystery
- ★ science fiction
- ★ biography
- ★ informational
- ★ poetry
- ★ graphic novel

Getting Ready (cont.)

Atmosphere (cont.)

Comfortable Reading Spaces

Comfortable reading spaces

> "While we may not have the comfortable setting of a hammock or the familiar front stoop, we can create a classroom atmosphere that invites everyone inside to pull up a piece of rug and settle into a good read."
>
> —Joanne Hindley (1996)

Just like us, children need places to curl up with a good book. These can be as elaborate as a permanent reading nook with a couch, comfortable chair, or child-size furnishings, or as simple as bean bag chairs and pillows, kept in a cabinet and dispersed at reading times.

Contain the Clutter

"Have a place for everything, and keep everything in its proper place" (Reverend C. A. Goodrich, 1827). This philosophy holds true for our classrooms.

Students read where they feel safe

Take inventory of the materials in your classroom. What is used regularly, sometimes, and rarely? Items used regularly should be stored within easy access. Materials used sometimes can be relocated to cabinets or shelves. If a resource is only used rarely (e.g., not used within the last three years), it needs to be purged. If you're not using it, it's clutter! The end result should place the focus on the instruction and not the room. Clutter, whether as materials in disarray, walls plastered with posters and charts, or bulletin boards in multiple colors and patterns, can be distracting to learning. Mess causes stress!

Adding More Ambiance

Place plants, water elements, potpourri (unless students are sensitive to it), or reed diffusers around the room. Quiet music playing during instruction creates a very desirable atmosphere. Music can also be used throughout the school day as transitional signals and to create a relaxed learning environment.

Organizational techniques

Getting Ready *(cont.)*

Book Boxes

Book Boxes

It used to be that students only kept one book at their desk to use during reading time. Teachers now know how important it is for children to have a variety of literature selections to stimulate their thinking and to keep them engaged while reading.

Just as an organized classroom has everything in its place, Book Boxes are the place where students keep text selections and reading tools.

Any reasonable container can work as a book basket: magazine files from office supply stores, baskets, and plastic ice cube bins. Remember to have enough for each student to have his or her own. Students will use them daily, so be mindful of accessibility, durability, and the storage space required and available.

These boxes store book selections, Reader's Notebooks, students' Tool Kits, and other reading essentials. Students can use them to easily transport all necessary materials to their favorite reading spot or book nook.

Young children should be guided in selecting how many and what types of books to have in their boxes. You might suggest that each student choose five books: one old favorite, one nonfiction, and three additional choices. Children choose new books weekly. Some teachers use Monday as their book shopping day for the class. Others have students make their book selections during their literacy work center rotation. A few have even incorporated book shopping into their morning routine. Book return methods can be just as varied. For example, assist the class by calling out the genre baskets categories. The students return those books, and then the teacher calls the next categories until all books are returned. Or, have students return the books on the day they have a conference with the teacher. You will ultimately find a method that works for you and your classroom.

Getting Ready (cont.)

Book Boxes (cont.)

There are some specific Book Box considerations that will support differentiation. We have distinguished them here by grade level:

Kindergarten

Book Box styles can vary at this age. Some teachers prefer baskets or box styles that are not as tall as magazine files. Students should only have 5–10 books in their boxes. These books should represent a variety of genres and readability levels.

Kindergarten Book Box

First Grade

Teacher preference plays a bigger role at this level in regards to box style. It all depends on what works for both teacher and students. Besides holding book selections, a number of teachers use the boxes to house Reader's Notebooks. If this is your choice, be careful to choose boxes that will accommodate your notebook size.

First or second grade Book Box

Second Grade

This is a transitional time for young readers. As they move from reading shorter stories to chapter books, guidelines for book quantities become more flexible and individualized to student needs. Maintain guidelines for genre diversity and readability. It becomes increasingly important for students to have "just right" reads in their Book Boxes at all times.

What is in your Tool Kit? Reading Tool Kits are not commercially purchased items, but are everyday materials used to enhance students' reading and understanding by helping them engage in rigorous thinking, organize ideas, and reflect about themselves as readers. A wide variety of tools are available, but the main ones teachers should use are listed on page 16.

Reading Tools

Reading Tool Kits

Students need to have the necessary reading supplies at their fingertips. Use a simple plastic bag or pencil pouch to hold the following: bookmarks, highlighter tape, sticky notes, and pencils. Throughout the lessons in this book, teachers introduce and model how each tool can be used. Students then practice during their independent reading time (see Composing Session, p. 28). As tools are introduced and implemented, add them to the tool kits.

Bookmarks

Students mark stopping places, track reading, or designate where learning and thinking transpired. We have included a template for a bookmark that can also be used to remind students of a decoding strategy (see Appendix C, p. 166). Fill in the blank bookmark with other strategy reminders.

Pencils

Sharpened pencils should be available at all times for a quick exchange to avoid sharpening of pencils during workshop time.

Sticky Notes

Students use these to flag or write about their thinking. The size and quantity of notes given to students differs by grade and teacher expectation. Start with five sticky notes. Students tend to overuse their notes at first, but with adequate modeling over time they will learn to be more judicious. *Note:* Try using a poster board for a sticky note "Parking Lot," which is useful when you want to assess student thinking and make them accountable for showing their use of the strategies.

Reading Tool Kit

Place student numbers or names on the chart and have students place their notes in that area to keep track of who has completed the assignment. This would be appropriate in first grade (later in the year) and second grade. (See Appendix B, p. 151, for an example of a "Parking Lot.")

Highlighter Tape

Students use tape to spotlight reading goals, such as finding letters, vowel patterns, high-frequency words, word families, unknown words, or other text features. Store the tape on a laminated card that has four lines drawn on it, one for each piece of tape (see Appendix C, p. 167). After using the highlighter tape, students should remove it from the book and replace it on the card. Tape left in books over time can become permanent. Children can check the lines to make sure they returned all of their tape pieces.

Getting Ready *(cont.)*

Reader's Notebooks

Reader's Notebooks have sections designed to help students as they engage with text. They serve as a continual record of the reader's thinking process during strategy work throughout the year. Teachers have used a variety of formats for these notebooks. Kindergarten teachers may prefer composition notebooks for young learners. Title pages are glued inside to create different sections. (For first and second grade, three-ring binders provide more flexibility. Clear-view covered binders work well.)

On the following pages, we describe the sections that can be used at each grade level.

Preparing Materials

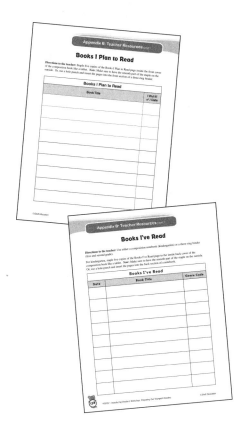

Reader's Notebook title pages and tabs should be copied on colored card stock for durability and to help designate sections (e.g., yellow card stock for title pages, orange card stock for Strategy Work, blue for Reflections). Be consistent with color choices for the entire class so you can direct students to "turn to the orange section for Strategy Work." If budget is an issue, use construction paper instead of card stock.

Other pages should be copied on regular paper.

Note: Since composition notebooks are a smaller size, adjust the sizes of the title pages to fit a 7" x $9\frac{1}{2}$" format.

Getting Ready (cont.)

Reader's Notebooks

Reader's Notebooks (cont.)

Assembling the Notebook

Cut out and glue the _____'s *Reader's Notebook* title on the front of the composition book, or slip it into the clear cover of a three-ring binder. Glue the *Strategy Work* title to the first page (or create a title page using card stock and a three-hole punch). In the center of the notebook where the stitched seam shows, glue the *Reading Reflections* title on the right-hand page (or use another piece of card stock to create a divider page).

To add the book logs, staple five copies of *Books I Plan to Read* pages inside the back cover like a tablet (or add five pages to the binder). Make sure to have the smooth part of the staple on the outside to avoid injuries and tablet damage. (First and second grade will include the *Books I've Read* log inside the front cover or in the front section of their binders.)

Note: In kindergarten, Reader's Notebooks may or may not be appropriate. You will need to evaluate your class each year to decide when and if you want to use them. You may want to start them in the middle of the year or you might feel like they may not be beneficial to your class at all.

Getting Ready *(cont.)*

Reader's Notebooks *(cont.)*

Books I Plan to Read

Kindergarten students read countless books throughout the week. Keep track of the books that the student would like to read. These can be recommendations from peers, new books in the library, or books they have seen other students reading. Students who write down those titles they want to read tend to follow through, and they love to check them off their lists after they have read them.

Kindergarten

Create the following title pages:

★ *Strategy Work*
★ *Reading Reflections*
★ *Books I Plan to Read*

Glue title pages into composition notebooks to differentiate the sections. Glue the *Strategy Work* title onto the first right-hand page. In the middle of the book (where the center seam shows), and on several pages afterward, glue the *Reading Reflections* title on the right-hand pages. Stack five or so copies of the *Books I Plan to Read* pages together to make a mini tablet. Staple those to the inside of the back cover. (Sample forms are provided in Appendix B, pp. 136–137 and p. 141, as well as on the Teacher Resource CD.)

Strategy Work

At this level, *Strategy Work* consists of students' illustrations. As students advance, they can begin to add writing to their drawings, or teachers can take a dictation. While teaching the thinking strategies, students will apply what they learned and translate those same strategies into words or illustrations in their Reader's Notebooks.

Reading Reflections

Within each lesson, students are asked to reflect on what they learned about themselves as readers. Students should always be thinking about what they are learning. For example, one of our students had drawn a girl with a book in her *Reading Reflections*. When the teacher took a dictation to add words to the picture, the student said, "I can read a book by looking at the pictures." There is no specific *Reading Reflection* template at this grade level. Students need space to draw a picture and lines below to add a commentary. It is up to the teacher to determine how to incorporate this piece into the session.

Getting Ready *(cont.)*

First grader's Reader's Notebook

Reader's Notebooks *(cont.)*

First Grade

First grade teachers will decide which type of Reader's Notebooks will work best—a composition book or a three-ring binder. After deciding, copy the appropriate title pages onto different colored card stock and insert them into the notebooks in the same way as described for kindergarten. (If you are using composition books, title pages will need to be cut down in size and the *Books I've Read* log will be stapled inside the front cover. Sample forms are provided in Appendix B, pp. 136–138 and p. 141, as well as on the Teacher Resource CD.)

Create the following title pages:
- ★ *Strategy Work*
- ★ *Reading Reflections* (several copies)
- ★ *Books I've Read*
- ★ *Books I Plan to Read*

Strategy Work

At this level, children should increase the amount of writing that goes with the pictures. For *Strategy Work,* students will highlight a comprehension strategy by writing what they find on a sticky note and then "parking" the note in the notebook for later elaboration.

Reading Reflections

Each week, students continue to reflect upon themselves as readers. This space provides a valuable tool for teachers to check and see if the students truly understand the strategies being taught.

Books I've Read

Once students are tracking all of the books they read, organize your library by genres with a genre code (NF = nonfiction, B = biography, A = award winning, etc.). Have students begin to identify what type of book they are reading and add that to their log sheets. This information can be useful to help guide students into other genres and expand their reading choices.

Books I Plan to Read

We hear of so many good books we really want to read. Have students jot down great book titles so they do not forget them. Children love to check off the book in the *I Did It!* column after they read it.

Getting Ready *(cont.)*

Reader's Notebooks *(cont.)*

Second Grade

Three-ring binders are a good option for this grade level. In this format, teachers have the flexibility to add sections and insert baseline charts to help guide student thinking and learning. When anchor charts are created during whole group instruction, they can be recreated by students in their notebooks if they are beneficial to student learning.

Note: Anchor charts are ongoing, so have students add new thinking to their charts throughout the year. Section titles should be printed on different colors of card stock for easy identification. Assemble the notebooks in a similar manner as for first grade and place the title pages in page protectors for extra durability (sample forms are provided in Appendix B, pp. 136–142. Create the following title pages:

★ *Books I've Read*
★ *Reading Resources*
★ *Strategy Work*
★ *Reading Response Letter and Rubric*
★ *Books I Plan to Read*

Books I've Read

Students keep track of their reading by genre. Periodically review students' logs to monitor their choices of different genres.

Reading Resources

These are baseline routines taught in the beginning phases of the Reader's Workshop model. Early mini-lessons at this level focus on "How to Choose a Book," "Book Genres," and "Book Basics." Chart replicas are copied by the students and added into their notebooks to reference.

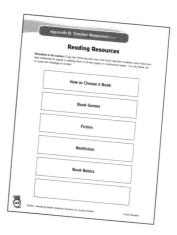

Reading Resources

Second grade libraries are organized with traditional genres. As you discuss these with students, create overview charts of the book traits you would expect in each group. Generate a genre code (NF = nonfiction, B = biography, HF = historical fiction, etc.). Have students add these genre codes to the *Reading Resources* section of their notebooks, under the tab "Book Genres" (see Appendix B, p. 142).

Getting Ready *(cont.)*

Reader's Notebooks *(cont.)*

Second Grade *(cont.)*

Strategy Work

Once students are writing regularly about their reading, focus on the specific comprehension strategy they are studying. As new strategies are introduced, anchor charts and thinking stem charts done in class can be copied and added here (McGregor 2007). Since some student thinking will be done on sticky notes, make sure to "park" the notes in the notebook, so their thinking is not lost. Second grade students should also begin using more scholarly language in their reading and writing.

Reading Response Letter and Rubric

Incorporate letter-writing skills with comprehension strategy instruction. This is another way for students to reflect upon their reading. Once or twice a month have students write a letter to the teacher discussing how they have grown as a reader, how they use the thinking strategy that is being taught at that time, or even perhaps questions that students have about themselves as readers or about the current strategy. Model a sample letter with the students to show them the proper format. This activity also reinforces basic letter writing skills and prepares students for creating reading logs. The sample letter is then added to their notebooks for reference. Letter format paper can be inserted for students to complete response letters. Teachers adjust the criteria as new skills are learned. We provide a 5 point rubric to evaluate the letters (Appendix B, p. 140), but any type of rubric can be created to meet the needs of students. Remember to reply to students. This is great way to build communication and rapport with your students, as well as provide valuable insights about their understanding.

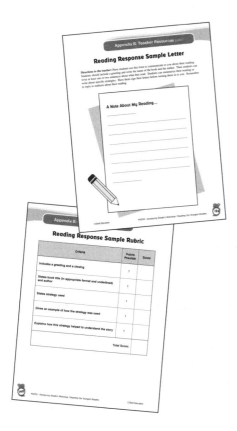

Books I Plan to Read

Have students list other books they are interested in, or recommendations they have received from peers.

Getting Ready (cont.)

Texts

Do you have a favorite children's book? Did it make you laugh or cry? Did it create pictures in your mind? That book would probably be a great choice to share for Reader's Workshop. The books that meant so much to you as a child are the ones that drew you in and created memories that have lasted a lifetime. Choose texts for your think-alouds that you love. Do not be concerned that these are your preferences; students will be drawn into your think-alouds because you shared a book that meant a great deal to you, and the authenticity of your choice will show.

During the first part of Reader's Workshop, you will need a variety of texts for strategy instruction. Though school and public libraries are great resources, start building a personal collection of old favorites that require deep comprehension. (Deep comprehension texts are those that cause the reader to go beyond literal comprehension by combining the text with the reader's own prior knowledge to construct understanding.) Deep comprehension helps students make suppositions as to why the events recounted in the text occurred, the probable effects of actions taken, the motives behind people's behavior, and the larger point made by the author of the text (McNamara 2007). Choose evocative books that speak to you—they should evoke memories, emotions, and wonders. A book that is perfect for one teacher might not be a good fit for another. It all has to do with schema, the memories and life experiences that a teacher brings when sharing the book.

Look for books that cause students to reflect and think beyond the story. Collect books that encourage metacognitive thinking and put them aside to introduce and model strategies throughout the year.

Great book lists can be found online and in the Recommended Reading section of this book (p. 173). Do not feel you must have a specific book to teach a strategy. Books go in and out of print and may not be available.

So, start with what you own, and gradually add titles. Keep your eye out for new books that endear themselves to you. New books can quickly become old favorites.

Anchor Charts

A variety of anchor charts will be created as a result of the lessons in this book. They should be purposely displayed throughout a Reader's Workshop classroom. Anchor charts are used to:

★ develop reading procedures and expectations
★ document student thinking
★ explain strategy instruction

For instance, an anchor chart can be a model to show students how to use sticky notes to document the places where a comprehension strategy was used while reading.

Anchor charts provide ongoing documentation of student thinking throughout the discussion of thinking strategies. They ensure that all children have access to a record of the growth and expansion in their thinking as a class. Due to space restraints, you may need to store some of these charts eventually, but make sure they are still accessible for students to reference and review.

How to Use This Book

Reader's Workshop is a ground breaking instructional framework in its ability to provide structure and explicit instruction without becoming rote or like a scripted program. Just as no two students are exactly alike, Reader's Workshop will look different from year to year and classroom to classroom. This book is designed with these qualities in mind. You will find specific and meaningful lessons to help students learn the basic routines and rituals necessary for a successful Reader's Workshop. However, some teachers might find that their students do not need as many lessons in one area, but do need extended time and work in another.

Effective teachers know that each new class is filled with students who have different learning styles and abilities. This variety will determine how a teacher might use this book. Also, students come into the classroom with different experiences and background knowledge. Teachers with students who have little school experience might find it beneficial to use all the lessons in this book, or even expand and repeat them as needed. If prekindergarten and kindergarten teachers are using this book school-wide, first and second grade may not need to complete each of the lessons due to their students' prior learning and school experiences. It might be more beneficial to use this book as a guide to refresh your students on the procedures essential to begin Reader's Workshop. Remember to spend as much time on each of the lessons as necessary for your classroom climate. This could mean repeating a lesson multiple times to ensure the procedures are in place.

The majority of this book is designed to assist teachers in providing the structure and routines essential for students to develop fundamental book and reading knowledge, reading stamina, and higher-level thinking skills. Do not mistake the teaching of these skills as Reader's Workshop. The lessons presented build crucial *foundations* for the rigorous work expected in the Reader's Workshop model.

This book offers explanations of the tools and important components needed to prepare for the Reader's Workshop model. Some of these structures will need to be put into practice prior to implementation, others during implementation, and a few procedures will be ongoing.

For example, prior to implementation, look at the physical room arrangement. Pay careful attention to delineated spaces for the four key areas: Large Group Meeting Spot, Small Group Meeting Spots, Reading Zones, and classroom library. There are many ways to organize a classroom library, but a well thought-out plan is vital. The room arrangement and atmosphere (lighting, comfortable reading spaces, etc.) should work together to create an intimate setting. Your environment should resonate with the message, "Reading is important!" This is the stage from which you will orchestrate the philosophical change of teaching children to read in a place where they feel safe and are willing to take risks.

How to Use This Book (cont.)

Planning Calendar

Each section begins with a five-lesson Planning Calendar. This overview provides a full agenda for the teacher, listing the lesson objectives and the materials needed. (Additional materials may be included within each individual lesson.) This overview allows the teacher to see the lessons "at a glance," showing where they are heading and what materials will be needed.

Also included is space for book selections and any additional notes that the teacher wants to make. Finally, the calendar allows space for the teacher to reflect on what went well and areas of improvement, keeping a record for future classrooms.

As you begin your exploration of the Planning Calendars, you may notice that the lessons are divided to accomplish separate goals. Each part is designed to be taught on the same day, but at different times. There should be extreme flexibility in these plans. If your students are ready, you can combine both lessons during one instructional period. If you are finding yourself short on time, teach the lessons on different days. If students do not seem to grasp the information or procedures, repeat the lesson until students have achieved mastery.

The two-part format provides the opportunity for shorter teaching periods, allowing even the youngest readers to stay focused. Instructional time must be utilized in the most beneficial way for children. Flexibility is always needed, and these lessons can be taught independently or together, depending on the makeup of your class. As you move into instruction, you may not find it necessary to teach every lesson, just as you may find that some lessons require additional time. The order of these lessons is not set in stone, but should serve as a guiding outline, allowing you to make choices and decisions in your instruction. The sequence of lessons allows your students to grow as readers. The lessons build upon one another so students will learn the skills and stamina needed for the Reader's Workshop model. Since every classroom is unique, you may need to adjust the timeline for your needs.

The last lessons of this book are meant to help build the structure to orchestrate strategy instruction. The lessons presented are offered as examples of how to introduce these strategies, and only represent some of the reading strategies that students will be exposed to in later grades. Lessons in each strategy can continue for several weeks as needed, or, if students are not ready for strategy instruction, review the earlier lessons instead. Strategies can be taught in any order, although you may find it makes sense to teach some strategies before others.

How to Use This Book *(cont.)*

Overview of Lesson Components

The lessons offer everything you need to plan ahead. We first show you the context for the lesson by identifying the standards and highlighting the lesson objectives. Planning guidelines will help you set up and successfully prepare for the lesson. The Procedure is broken into the Crafting, Composing, and Reflection sessions.

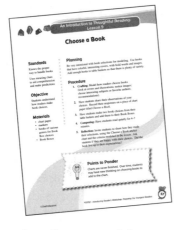

The Crafting Session outlines the main points of the lesson. Some suggested phrasing is provided, but it is meant merely as an example and should not be used as a rote script. You select your own book titles according to your personal preference and the specific requirements of your students.

During the Composing Session, students work independently, in pairs, or in small groups, applying the strategies that have been demonstrated.

The lessons conclude with Reflection, where students are asked to reflect on their own learning.

At the end of each lesson are Points to Ponder, which may offer ideas for differentiation, or simply a helpful management tip. Just as we ask students to reflect upon their learning, you, too, will want to be metacognitive and record your thinking about the lesson. Remember, space for reflection is provided in each Planning Calendar. (A more detailed description of each lesson component is found on pp. 27–30.)

Finally, Appendices are included with templates for the materials used in the lessons. Think of these examples like a picture on a puzzle box. Being able to visualize the final product will help you put the pieces together with greater ease. Our teachers have made adjustments over time to make them their own, and we encourage you to do the same. You will also find these templates on the Teacher Resource CD. (See p. 175 for the contents of the Teacher Resource CD.)

The lesson components are woven into a predictable format for implementing strategy instruction easily. There are guidelines and time frames listed when appropriate, which will be especially important as you plan instruction. Text selection for your Crafting sessions should be a deliberate process. It is not enough to select a favorite book. Find books that are thought-provoking, that will cause children to change how they think about themselves and the world. Space for book selections is available on the Planning Calendars, and a short list of our favorites is provided in the Recommended Reading section on p. 173.

The Recommended Reading also lists professional resources, though our list represents only a fraction of the titles available to further your understanding. These key texts will at least start you toward deeper, more thoughtful reading instruction as the vital components of the Reader's Workshop model fall into place. Continue the intellectual journey by adding to your knowledge base and broadening your understanding of how to better teach children to read. Your goal is to create a love of reading that will sustain students for a lifetime.

How to Use This Book *(cont.)*

Overview of Lesson Components *(cont.)*

Once the groundwork has been laid, you are ready to put Reader's Workshop into practice. Your students will gradually be prepared for explicit strategy instruction. These thinking strategies are discussed in depth in research on proficient readers, and synthesized by Pearson et al. (1992). They include: metacognition, monitoring for meaning, activating schema, making mental images (or visualizing), inferring, asking questions, determining importance, and synthesizing.

Reader's Workshop is a structure that supports the instruction of the comprehension or thinking strategies. (See Transition into Strategy Instruction on p. 30.) Strategy instruction begins after you have finished building Reader's Workshop routines and getting your students comfortable as readers. The key elements of the components for the Reader's Workshop model are described in Ellin Keene's books *To Understand* (2008) and *Mosaic of Thought* (Keene and Zimmerman 1997; 2007). This information should be useful as you begin the transition toward implementing Reader's Workshop in your classroom. The following elements are described in Keene's work *To Understand*. We summarize the key features here:

Crafting Session

Reader's Workshop begins with the Crafting Session, when the teacher introduces or models his or her own thinking. Since most of the modeling and strategy instruction is done at this time, it is important to keep the attention span of the learners in mind. Usually 10 to 20 minutes will suffice, depending on student stamina and grade level.

The following are some key points to keep in mind for the Crafting Session:

★ Gather students three to five times a week in the Large Group Meeting Spot.

★ Use rituals such as music, bells, or tones to call students to the meeting spot.

★ Think aloud, model, and demonstrate how to use strategies.

★ Select text that is evocative and conducive to thinking aloud—the literature you choose is fundamental to the success of the lesson.

★ Limit the focus of the lesson to one teaching objective (unless the goal is to link the lesson to previously learned material). Ask yourself, "What is my objective?" and stick to it.

★ Have students complete meaningful, independent work. Students should be able to leave the lesson with a reading goal in mind.

How to Use This Book (cont.)

Composing Session

While the Crafting Session focuses on instruction, the Composing Session focuses on student application. This is when students are reading independently or in pairs with books of their choice. The teacher's role is to confer with individual students or meet with invitational groups. During the Composing sessions, try to achieve the following:

★ Allow students time to read independently so you can conference with individual students regarding their application of recently taught deep-structure (meaning and comprehension) or surface-structure (word decoding and fluency) strategies.

★ Offer opportunities for students to meet in book clubs to discuss books that they have all read and how they applied deep- and surface-structure strategies.

★ Allow time to plan with students (in individual conferences or with groups) what they could share during the Reflection. Allow from 30 to 45 minutes for independent work at the primary level. Start slowly and build up to longer periods of independent reading.

Conferring

This is the time when a teacher is able to differentiate instruction to meet the needs of all learning styles and levels. The first goal when conferring is to gain knowledge of the student as a reader. When you have a good grasp on students' abilities, you are able to instruct them in a way that will make them better readers. This is the ultimate goal of conferring.

The following are some key points to keep in mind when conferring:

★ Before starting conferences, stand back and observe the classroom to determine if someone needs special attention. Decide who is ready for independent work and who may need more guidance.

★ Use a conferring notebook to keep track of students' thinking, goal setting, and learning (see sample layouts for a conferring notebook, as well as descriptions of how to use them, in Appendix B, pp. 145–146).

★ Circulate among students. More students can be involved in the learning by listening as you conference with another.

★ For deep-structure conferences, provide students with challenging books; for surface-structure conferences, use leveled text.

★ Students do not have to read aloud during deep-structure conferences. You can read to them. Confer with a book at your side.

★ Always center your discussion around the idea of how this strategy helps to better understand the text. Be sure the student understands how this strategy helps him or her become a better reader.

★ Conferences for these grade levels should focus 50 percent on surface structure and 50 percent on deep structure.

★ Minimize interruptions by waiting to address the problems or needs of other students.

How to Use This Book (cont.)

Overview of Lesson Components (cont.)

Conferring (cont.)

As you confer with students, your confidence will grow and you will create a system and routine that works for you. To ensure effectiveness, create a predictable routine. During a conference, you should be reflecting on what you can teach this student, right here and now, that will boost the student's confidence as a reader higher than before the conference.

Next, decide if this student's challenge is something that the whole class would benefit from experiencing. If so, then prepare the student to teach his or her metacognitive strategy to the class as part of Reflection.

The conference ends when you give the student a goal to work toward before the next conference. Keep track of students' goals in your conferring notebook.

During the conference, note the following:

★ Check the student's progress toward the previous goal (from the last conference with the student).

★ Have the student demonstrate the skill taught during the Crafting Session.

★ Have the student demonstrate mastery of a previously taught skill.

Invitational Groups

The teacher uses information from the conferring notebook to form needs-based groups for intensive instruction on a particular skill or strategy, either in the form of remediation or enrichment. Unlike fixed, ability-based groups, invitational groups are constantly changing as a teacher notices students who have similar needs. Keep the following key objectives in mind when forming invitational groups:

★ Select students who will benefit from the opportunity to observe you model in a more controlled, focused setting than in a large group.

★ Select students who will benefit from your close observation as you model a deep- or surface-structure strategy again, and ask students to apply what they learn.

★ Choose students who are ready to go to a higher level of text to extend their thinking.

★ If there is a surface-structure skill or strategy that most of the class demonstrates independently, which students need this skill or strategy reinforced?

★ Consider choosing students who need immediate attention as they read and discuss problems they encounter.

Invitational groups meet during the Composing sessions. This replaces their conferring time for the day.

How to Use This Book *(cont.)*

Overview of Lesson Components *(cont.)*

Reflection

This final piece of Reader's Workshop is always the last step of the lesson procedures and turns the role of teaching over to the students. By talking to individual students about what they learned about themselves as readers, the teacher sees who is prepared to share the strategies that helped them as readers. The goal is for this information to assist other students. Students can teach their peers the basic skills they used to assist their reading or the strategies they used to aid their understanding. The following ideas will help you facilitate a productive Reflection Session:

★ Seat students in a circle or oval shape, usually on the floor, so they can see each other easily.

★ Demonstrate for the students how they can "teach" others during the Reflection session.

★ Have each student focus on these questions: "What did I learn about myself as a reader?" and "What can I share that will help other readers?"

★ Instruct students to challenge what is shared and argue diplomatically with the reflecting child and other students.

Transition into Strategy Instruction

Once you have the components and the initial procedures in place, students will be ready to move into strategy instruction. The comprehension strategies of metacognition, monitoring for meaning, visualizing, activating schema, asking questions, predicting or inferring, determining importance, and synthesizing will help your students continue to grow as readers. The last 10 lessons are transitional lessons designed to introduce these strategies using books from the reading list. In Appendix B (p. 144) and on the Teacher Resource CD, you will find icons to symbolize each strategy. Place these icons on activity pages or enlarge them to attach to your bulletin board. These will provide a visual reference for younger students, and remind older students about the overall goal of each thinking strategy.

How to Use This Book (cont.)

Overview of Lesson Components (cont.)

Transition into Strategy Instruction (cont.)

Icon	Strategy	Definition
	Metacognition	• think about your thinking • know that reading is thinking
	Monitor for Meaning	• know when you no longer understand the text • have ways to check understanding • know your purpose for reading
	Visualize	• create pictures in your mind using the author's words • find sensory images that allow you to see, hear, taste, smell, and feel
	Ask Questions	• before, during, and after reading to increase understanding of the text
	Activate Schema	• have an enhanced understanding because of something that you know, feel, or have seen before • create new schema from the author's words
	Predict/Infer	• use the author's words and your own schema to form conclusions that are not explicitly stated
	Determine Importance	• decide what is important and what needs to be remembered
	Synthesize	• change and adjust your thinking as you read • put the pieces together to get the big picture

Correlation to Standards

Shell Education is committed to producing educational materials that are research and standards based. In this effort, we have correlated all of our products to the academic standards of all 50 states, the District of Columbia, and the Department of Defense Dependent Schools.

How to Find Standards Correlations

To print a customized correlation report of this product for your state, visit our website at **http://www.shelleducation.com** and follow the on-screen directions. If you require assistance in printing correlation reports, please contact Customer Service at 1-877-777-3450.

Purpose and Intent of Standards

The No Child Left Behind legislation mandates that all states adopt academic standards that identify the skills students will learn in kindergarten through grade twelve. While many states had already adopted academic standards prior to NCLB, the legislation set requirements to ensure the standards were detailed and comprehensive.

Standards are designed to focus instruction and guide adoption of curricula. Standards are statements that describe the criteria necessary for students to meet specific academic goals. They define the knowledge, skills, and content students should acquire at each level. Standards are also used to develop standardized tests to evaluate students' academic progress.

Teachers are required to demonstrate how their lessons meet state standards. State standards are used in development of all of our products, so educators can be assured they meet the academic requirements of each state.

McREL Compendium

We use the Mid-continent Research for Education and Learning (McREL) Compendium to create standards correlations. Each year, McREL analyzes state standards and revises the compendium. By following this procedure, McREL is able to produce a general compilation of national standards. Each lesson in this product is based on one or more McREL standards. The chart on pages 33–34 lists each standard taught in this product and the page numbers for the corresponding lessons.

TESOL Standards

The lessons in this book promote English language development for English Language Support. The standards listed on page 35 support the language objectives presented throughout the lessons.

Correlation to Standards (cont.)

Standard	Lesson and Page Number
Knows the proper way to handle books	Lesson 1, pp. 38–39; Lesson 2, pp. 40–41; Lesson 9, pp. 56–57
Understands rules and the purposes they serve	Lesson 1, pp. 38–39; Lesson 2, pp. 40–41; Lesson 3, pp. 42–43; Lesson 4, pp. 44–45; Lesson 12, pp. 64–65; Lesson 13, pp. 66–67; Lesson 14, pp. 68–69; Lesson 20, pp. 82–83; Lesson 25, pp. 94–95; Lesson 32, pp. 112–113
Uses emergent skills to "read" a story	Lesson 2, pp. 40–41; Lesson 3, pp. 42–43; Lesson 4, pp. 44–45; Lesson 12, pp. 64–65; Lesson 16, pp. 74–75
Understands that illustrations and pictures convey meaning	Lesson 2, pp. 40–41; Lesson 3, pp. 42–43; Lesson 10, pp. 58–59; Lesson 13, pp. 66–67; Lesson 14, pp. 68–69; Lesson 16, pp. 74–75
Uses language to communicate thoughts, feelings, and needs	Lesson 5, pp. 46–47; Lesson 15, pp. 70–71
Demonstrates respect for others' rights and feelings	Lesson 5, pp. 46–47
Actively listens to the key ideas of others and asks clarifying questions	Lesson 6, pp. 50–51; Lesson 7, pp. 52–53
Knows familiar print in the environment	Lesson 6, pp. 50–51; Lesson 7, pp. 52–53; Lesson 8, pp. 54–55
Knows that print and written symbols convey meaning and represent spoken language	Lesson 7, pp. 52–53; Lesson 8, pp. 54–55
Knows strategies to effectively communicate in a variety of settings	Lesson 8, pp. 54–55
Uses meaning clues to aid comprehension and make predictions about content	Lesson 9, pp. 56–57; Lesson 13, pp. 66–67; Lesson 14, pp. 68–69; Lesson 16, pp. 74–75; Lesson 33, pp. 114–115; Lesson 34, pp.116–117; Lesson 41, p. 130; Lesson 42, p. 131
Exhibits care for personal belongings and school materials	Lesson 10, pp. 58–59; Lesson 11, pp. 62–63; Lesson 13, pp. 66–67; Lesson 34, pp. 116–117; Lesson 35, pp. 118–119
Knows that books have titles, authors, and often illustrators	Lesson 10, pp. 58–59; Lesson 11, pp. 62–63; Lesson 12, pp. 64–65
Demonstrates appropriate behaviors for relating well with others	Lesson 11, pp. 62–63; Lesson 12, pp. 64–65; Lesson 17, pp. 76–77; Lesson 18, pp. 78–79; Lesson 19, pp. 80–81; Lesson 24, pp. 92–93; Lesson 27, pp. 100–101; Lesson 28, pp. 102–103; Lesson 29, pp. 104–105; Lesson 30, pp. 106–107; Lesson 31, pp. 110–111
Knows the difference between fact and fiction, real and make-believe	Lesson 13, pp. 66–67; Lesson 14, pp. 68–69; Lesson 15, pp. 70–71; Lesson 16, pp. 74–75

Correlation to Standards *(cont.)*

Standard	Lesson and Page Number
Relates new information to prior knowledge and experiences	Lesson 17, pp. 76–77; Lesson 37, p. 123; Lesson 38, p. 124; Lesson 40, p. 126; Lesson 43, p. 132
Knows that print is read from left to right	Lesson 18, pp. 78–79; Lesson 19, pp. 80–81; Lesson 20, pp. 82–83
Follows one- and two-step directions	Lesson 20, pp. 81–82
Knows the basic characteristics of familiar genres	Lesson 21, pp. 86–87; Lesson 22, pp. 88–89; Lesson 23, pp. 90–91; Lesson 26, pp. 98–99
Knows setting, main characters, main events, sequence, narrator, and problems in stories	Lesson 21, pp. 86–87; Lesson 22, pp. 88–89; Lesson 23, pp. 90–91; Lesson 25, pp. 94–95; Lesson 26, pp. 98–99; Lesson 27, pp. 100–101; Lesson 29, pp. 104–105; Lesson 30, pp. 106–107; Lesson 32, pp. 112–113; Lesson 33, pp. 114–115; Lesson 35, pp. 118–119
Knows the main idea or theme of a story, drama, or poem	Lesson 22, pp. 88–89; Lesson 23, pp. 90–91; Lesson 25, pp. 94–95; Lesson 26, pp. 98–99; Lesson 29, pp. 104–105; Lesson 31, pp. 110–111
Uses reading skills and strategies to understand a variety of familiar literary text	Lesson 22, pp. 88–89; Lesson 26, pp. 98–99
Predicts story events or outcome using illustrations and prior knowledge as a guide	Lesson 28, pp. 102–103
Asks questions to obtain information	Lesson 36, p. 122; Lesson 38, p. 124; Lesson 39, p. 125; Lesson 41, p. 130
Uses mental images based on pictures and print to aid in comprehension of text	Lesson 36, p. 122; Lesson 37, p. 123; Lesson 38, p. 124; Lesson 39, p. 125; Lesson 41, p. 130
Relates stories to personal experiences	Lesson 31, pp. 110–111; Lesson 36, p. 122; Lesson 39, p. 125; Lesson 40, p. 126; Lesson 43, p. 132
Uses visual and verbal clues, including pictures, to comprehend new words and stories	Lesson 45, p. 134
Follows classroom rules and routines	Lesson 35, p. 118
Uses self-correction strategies	Lesson 42, p. 131
Understands the main idea and supporting details of simple expository information	Lesson 44, p. 133

Correlation to Standards *(cont.)*

TESOL Chart

Standard	Lesson	Page Number
To use English to communicate in social settings: Students will use English to participate in social interactions	All lessons	38–134
Students will interact in, through, and with spoken and written English for personal expression and enjoyment	All lessons	38–134
Students will use learning strategies to extend their communicative competence	All lessons	38–134
To use English to achieve academically in all content areas: Students will use English to interact in the classroom	All lessons	38–134
Students will use English to obtain, process, construct, and provide subject matter information in spoken and written form	All lessons	38–134
Students will use appropriate learning strategies to construct and apply academic knowledge	All lessons	38–134
To use English in socially and culturally appropriate ways: Students will use the appropriate language variety, register, and genre according to audience, purpose, and setting	All lessons	38–134
Students will use nonverbal communication appropriate to audience, purpose, and setting	All lessons	38–134
Students will use appropriate learning strategies to extend their sociolinguistic and sociocultural competence	All lessons	38–134

Planning Calendar

	Lesson 1	**Lesson 2**	**Lesson 3**
Part 1	**Signal for Coming to the Carpet** Establish procedures for coming to the Meeting Spot **Materials** a "coming to the carpet" signal	**Introduce the Meeting Spot** Review procedures for coming to the Large Group Meeting Spot **Materials** none	**Meeting Spot Behaviors** Establish expected behaviors at the Meeting Spot **Materials** chart paper; markers
Part 2	**Book Care** Recognize and understand appropriate book care **Materials** basket of damaged books; chart paper; markers	**Ways to Read a Book** Learn different ways to read a book (read the pictures, read the words) **Materials** picture book for model lesson; books for students to read	**Retell a Book** Learn another way to read a book by retelling a story **Materials** familiar picture book; chart paper; markers; books for students to read
Preparation	Book selections: Notes:	Book selections: Notes:	Book selections: Notes:

Planning Calendar

Lesson 4	Lesson 5	Reflection
More Meeting Spot Behaviors Refine expected behavior for the Meeting Spot **Materials** Expected Behaviors anchor chart; markers	**Respectful Manners and Language** Establish respectful manners and language **Materials** chart paper; markers	**What went well?** _____ _____ _____ _____ _____ _____ _____ _____
Read Quietly Read quietly so as not to disturb others and allow them to think **Materials** books for students to read	**Maintain a Quiet Environment** Practice maintaining a quiet reading environment **Materials** chart paper; markers; books for students; Three Ways to Read anchor chart	_____ _____ _____ **Areas for improvement:** _____ _____ _____
Book selections:	**Book selections:**	_____ _____ _____ _____
Notes:	**Notes:**	_____ _____ _____ _____

Signal for Coming to the Carpet

Standard

Understands rules and the purposes they serve

Objective

Teacher establishes procedures for coming to the Large Group Meeting Spot.

Materials

- a "come to the carpet" signal

Planning

Determine your cue for students to come to the carpet (a hand signal, special song, a bell, etc.). Determine how you want the students to sit. Will they have predetermined spots? Is there a specific posture they should take?

Procedure

1. **Crafting:** Demonstrate exactly how you want your students to perform this procedure.

2. Have one or two students practice the procedure in front of the class.

3. Have students discuss what went well or might need to be adjusted.

4. **Composing:** Have students work in small groups to practice until the entire class is at the meeting spot.

5. Choose one or two students to lead the class. After a few days, choose another set of volunteers until every student has had a chance to be a leader.

6. **Reflection:** Pay attention to problems such as students wanting to reserve a spot or two students arguing over the same space. Ask students to problem-solve how to create space for everyone.

Points to Ponder

This procedure will be part of your daily routine. Depending on the dynamics of your class and schedule, you may choose to practice this lesson for several days before moving on to Book Care.

Book Care

Standard

Knows the proper way to handle books

Objective

Students practice how to recognize and understand appropriate book care, using damaged books as examples.

Materials

- basket of damaged books
- chart paper
- markers

Planning

Determine guidelines for book care and create a space on your bulletin board for a poster with pictures to remind students. Set up a designated spot for damaged books that need repair.

Procedure

1. **Crafting:** Hold up a damaged book. Ask students, "What do you think happened to this book?" Students may notice torn pages, markings, or stains.

2. Explain that books in the classroom belong to everyone, including future students; therefore, each student shares the responsibility of keeping books in good condition.

3. **Composing:** Ask a student to show the class how to appropriately handle a book. Ask students for other ideas, such as making sure your hands are clean and dry; using a bookmark to keep your place; returning books to the shelves; and handling pages and covers gently. Label a chart *Book Care* for recording and displaying students' suggestions.

4. **Reflection:** Ask students to reflect on one thing they want to remember about how to handle books to keep them in good condition.

Points to Ponder

You may want to designate a special place for damaged books. Catchy names like "Our Book Hospital" or "Repair Center" are always fun.

Introduce the Meeting Spot

Standard

Understands rules and the purposes they serve

Objective

Students practice procedures for coming to the Large Group Meeting Spot.

Materials

- none

Planning

Identify the successful elements of the Coming to the Carpet Signal lesson. Let students know that they will be given many opportunities to practice the procedure. Determine if any adjustments are needed and be prepared to bring up your concerns.

Procedure

1. **Crafting:** Remind students of the Coming to the Carpet signal. Ask several students to explain what the signal is and what it means.

2. Designate a specific place for the Meeting Spot. Choose a name for the area, and refer to it in the agenda so students understand where they are to meet when asked to go there.

3. **Composing:** Ask a student volunteer to demonstrate how to come and sit at the meeting spot. Ask other students if there is anything that was forgotten from the previous day.

4. Ask all students to practice several times. This can be a game, with students trying to improve in speed and proficiency. Continue to practice as necessary.

5. **Reflection:** Ask students to share the steps for coming to the Meeting Spot.

Points to Ponder

To keep the process orderly, assign numbers to table groups, and ask only one group to come to the meeting spot at a time.

#50702 —Introducing Reader's Workshop: Preparing Our Youngest Readers

Ways to Read a Book

Standards

Uses emergent reading skills to "read" a story

Understands that illustrations and pictures convey meaning

Knows the proper way to handle books

Objective

Students practice different ways to read a book (e.g., read the pictures, read the words).

Materials

- picture book for model lesson
- books for students to read

Planning

Decide how many books you want in each table basket (e.g., three or more per child). When and how will you pass out book baskets to each group? Choose a student from each group to be book monitor. (Rotate book monitors regularly.)

Procedure

1. **Crafting:** Model how to read a story by using only the pictures. Point to details in the pictures that demonstrate foreshadowing or that help students make predictions.

2. Read the same book using the words. Ask students if the words made a difference to the story. How did the words contribute to their understanding?

3. Have a few student volunteers demonstrate both ways to read a book. Discuss the importance of having different ways to read books.

4. **Composing:** Have students read books with partners, using both ways for 3–5 minutes.

5. **Reflection:** Ask students what they did to understand the stories they read. Ask for volunteers to explain to the class how they read their book.

Points to Ponder

In first and second grades, students will possess a higher reading stamina. If students are ready to read for longer periods, they should be allowed to do so.

Meeting Spot Behaviors

Standard

Understand rules and purposes they serve

Objective

Teacher establishes expected behaviors for students when they are at the Large Group Meeting Spot.

Materials

- chart paper
- markers

Planning

Identify the exact student behaviors needed for the meeting spot (e.g., sit on your bottom, keep your hands to yourself, keep your eyes on the teacher, listen for the attention signal). Analyze the specific steps necessary to teach the desired behaviors. Leave nothing to chance. Be very deliberate in your instruction.

Procedure

1. **Crafting:** Discuss and model expected behaviors. Teach each behavior individually, and limit the expectations to two or three behaviors. As students are comfortable, more behaviors can be included. Label a chart *Expected Behaviors,* and write down expectations that have been discussed.

2. **Composing:** Ask a student volunteer to demonstrate each behavior.

3. Review and practice the expected behaviors frequently.

4. **Reflection:** Point to one of the expected behaviors listed on the chart and ask a student to demonstrate that behavior. Ask students to tell how using the expected behavior helped the class run efficiently. Keep the chart clearly visible during instruction.

Points to Ponder

Maintain a high level of expectation for student behavior at the meeting spot. The standards you set in place now will impact the effectiveness of your lessons for the entire year. Prepare to practice this lesson often.

Retell a Book

Standards

Understands that illustrations and pictures convey meaning

Uses emergent reading skills to "read" a story

Objective

Students learn another way to read a book by retelling a story.

Materials

- familiar picture book
- chart paper
- markers
- books for students to read

Planning

Choose a story you have read to the class before. Make sure it has interesting details, is well-known, and has a familiar story line. Plan out the points you want to emphasize ahead of time so you know where to elaborate when retelling the story.

Procedure

1. **Crafting:** Explain that students will learn another way to read a book. Tell them that you will retell a story they have heard many times before.

2. Retell a story from a previous day from memory, highlighting the plot, characters, and main events. Ask students to add any other details they remember.

3. Label a chart *Three Ways to Read*, and draw three columns. Label the columns: *Using Pictures*, *Reading the Words*, and *Retelling from Memory*.

4. Ask students to name the key points of each technique. Add their ideas to the anchor chart.

5. **Composing:** Have students read independently for 3–5 minutes. Direct them to practice all three methods.

6. **Reflection:** Ask students to pick their favorite method of reading a book, and to tell why.

Points to Ponder

If some students have difficulty retelling stories, try using familiar fairy tales, nursery rhymes, and songs until they feel more comfortable with the process.

More Meeting Spot Behaviors

Standard

Understands rules and purposes they serve

Objective

Students refine expected behaviors for the Large Group Meeting Spot.

Materials

- Expected Behaviors anchor chart (Lesson 3, p. 42)
- markers

Planning

Reflect on students' behavior when they are at the Meeting Spot. Are there any new behaviors or expectations that need to be addressed? Have there been any conflicts or special circumstances that have been preventing the students from meeting the expectations for behavior? Encourage students to bring up any issues they may be having.

Procedure

1. **Crafting:** Ask students to share why it is important to have expected behaviors (gives every student a turn to talk, no one gets injured or has hurt feelings).

2. Explain that it is important to revisit expectations and even to add some new expectations if circumstances call for it. Discuss one or two new behavior problems and ask students to brainstorm some ways to handle these issues.

3. Model the new expectations.

4. **Composing:** Ask student volunteers to demonstrate the new behaviors.

5. **Reflection:** Practice the expected behaviors as a class. Add the new guidelines to the anchor chart.

Points to Ponder

Think of a good place to display the anchor chart so that you and your students can reference it often. Anchor charts are never finished. Teach and add additional expectations as necessary.

Read Quietly

Standards

Uses emergent reading skills to "read" a story

Understands rules and purposes they serve

Objective

Students learn how to read quietly so as not to disturb others and to allow them to think.

Materials

- books for students to read

Planning

Think of situations when loud noises disturbed your thinking. Include situations that the students may encounter, such as loud talking or singing, tapping pencils, kicking chairs, or loud music.

Procedure

1. **Crafting:** Tell students that reading is thinking and often our best thinking happens when it is quiet. For independent reading, students will need to read quietly so as not to interrupt anyone's thinking. Ask students to share conditions that help them do their best thinking.

2. Model reading quietly by moving your lips without making sound, and putting your finger on the words to keep your place. Have several students demonstrate quiet, independent reading. Ask students what they noticed or how successfully they thought these students were able to read quietly.

3. **Composing:** Have students practice reading independently at their seats for 4–7 minutes.

4. **Reflection:** Ask students how a quiet classroom can help them as readers.

Points to Ponder

Soft music can set a hushed tone for your room during quiet reading. Use music that has a moderate and consistent tempo, without lyrics. Also, a steady hum from an appliance such as a fan may be helpful background noise.

Respectful Manners and Language

Standard

Uses language to communicate thoughts, feelings, and needs

Objective

Teacher establishes respectful manners and language.

Materials

- chart paper
- markers

Planning

Identify key polite words that students should use during the call-and-response lesson (e.g., *thank you*, *please*, *excuse me*).

Procedure

1. **Crafting:** Discuss with students how using polite words could help the classroom, especially during Reader's Workshop (e.g., polite words allow everyone to feel as if their ideas are respected).

2. Have students call out polite words and list them on a chart labeled *We Speak Politely*. Ask students when these words would be used (e.g., to interrupt).

3. Model the call-and-response format by asking students to share any polite words that he or she knows. Each student should respond with a comment such as, "I know the words *thank you*."

4. **Composing:** Have students demonstrate the call-and-response format by choosing a peer to call and respond to; continue for several turns.

5. **Reflection:** Ask students how it feels to use and hear polite words. Encourage students to elaborate, rather than just labeling their feelings. Record their ideas in the anchor chart.

Points to Ponder

Insist that students address each other by name. Discuss impolite words and behavior to show both examples and nonexamples. Role-playing is another good option. Behavior etiquette is essential to set the tone of the classroom and should be used daily.

#50702 –Introducing Reader's Workshop: Preparing Our Youngest Readers

Maintain a Quiet Environment

Standard

Demonstrates respect for others' rights and feelings

Objective

Students practice maintaining a quiet reading environment.

Materials

- chart paper
- markers
- books for students
- Three Ways to Read anchor chart (Lesson 3, p. 43)

Planning

Prepare examples of what quiet reading sounds like (pages turning softly; students using inside voices; low music playing; students whispering, "Sh-sh-sh … I'm reading").

Procedure

1. **Crafting:** Remind students how to be book responsible, the three ways to read a book, and why it is important to read quietly.

2. Draw a two-column T-chart on a sheet of chart paper, and title it *Looks Like, Sounds Like*. Label the left column *Quiet Reading Looks Like…*, and the right column *Quiet Reading Sounds Like…*. Ask students to help you fill in each column with words or drawings.

3. **Composing:** Have students practice quiet reading for 4–7 minutes. Remind students that reading quietly allows others to think as they read.

4. **Reflection:** Use the call-and-response format to ask students how it helped to have the people around them reading quietly. Did they notice anyone using any of the behaviors listed on the T-chart?

Points to Ponder

Have students give compliments to neighbors regarding reading behaviors. This is just one more way to add to their respectful etiquette repertoire.

Planning Calendar

	Lesson 6	Lesson 7	Lesson 8
Part 1	**Listening Behavior** Develop active listening behaviors **Materials** We Speak Politely anchor chart	**Active Listening** Learn manners and language etiquette **Materials** We Speak Politely anchor chart; markers	**Patience and Polite Words** Review manners and language etiquette **Materials** We Speak Politely anchor chart
Part 2	**What Readers Read** Recognize that reading is all around them **Materials** environmental print; books for students	**Review of What Readers Read** Students view themselves as readers **Materials** chart paper; markers; glue or stapler; environmental print; books for students	**I Can Read…** Practice reading environmental print **Materials** I Can Read… anchor chart; book baskets
Preparation	Book selections: Notes:	Book selections: Notes:	Book selections: Notes:

Planning Calendar

Lesson 9	Lesson 10	Reflection
How to Handle a Book Box Develop Book Box handling skills	**Work with Book Boxes** Develop organizational skills for keeping Book Boxes neat and tidy	**What went well?** _____ _____ _____ _____ _____ _____ _____
Materials Book Care anchor chart; one Book Box	**Materials** messy backpack; chart paper; markers; Book Boxes	_____ _____ _____ _____
Choose a Book Understand how readers make book choices	**Book Box Choices** Practice how to choose a book to add to Book Boxes	
Materials chart paper; markers; Book Boxes; books of various genres	**Materials** Choose a Book anchor chart; markers; books of various genres; Book Boxes	**Areas for improvement:** _____ _____ _____
Book selections:	**Book selections:**	_____ _____ _____ _____
Notes:	**Notes:**	_____ _____ _____ _____ _____

Listening Behavior

Standard

Actively listens to the key ideas of others and asks clarifying questions

Objective

Students develop active listening behavior.

Materials

- We Speak Politely anchor chart (Lesson 5, p. 46)

Planning

Determine what it means to be an *active listener* (focus attention on the speaker, communicate a message back in your own words, maintain eye contact and appropriate body language).

Procedure

1. **Crafting:** Introduce the term *active listener* and describe what it looks like to be an active listener during Reader's Workshop (e.g., an active listener looks at the speaker and waits until the speaker finishes talking before raising his or her hand or responding).

2. Model with a student how active listeners conduct themselves during a conversation (e.g., eye contact, smiling, body position). Refer to the We Speak Politely anchor chart.

3. **Composing:** Role-play scenarios that demonstrate appropriate and inappropriate listening behaviors. Have students identify the appropriate behaviors.

4. **Reflection:** Using the call-and-response format, ask several students to share how they can demonstrate that they are active listeners.

Points to Ponder

Active listening is a lifelong skill that students should learn as early as possible. Students will be applying active listening skills in all components of Reader's Workshop. Spend as much time as necessary for students to master active listening.

What Readers Read

Standard

Knows familiar print in their environment

Objective

Students recognize that reading is all around them.

Materials

- environmental print (candy wrappers, street signs, food labels)
- books for students

Planning

Be sure there are signs and posters easily visible around the room. Think about posting pictures of familiar signs or examples of print found around the campus.

Procedure

1. **Crafting:** Point out environmental print in the classroom or use samples you collected. Show students how signs around the room help to find things.

2. Discuss other things people read (newspapers, food wrappers, or instructions) using the respectful call-and-response format (described in Lesson 5, p. 46).

3. Have students bring samples of environmental print to school. Brainstorm some possible examples that students could select.

4. **Composing:** Have students practice quiet reading at their seats for 4–7 minutes.

5. **Reflection:** Use the call-and-response format to ask students to share a favorite word they read.

Points to Ponder

Take an environmental print field trip around the school. Have students identify all the things they can read. Initially, you will need to model the exact language you would like students to use until students take ownership of the language and use it automatically.

Active Listening

Standard

Actively listens to the key ideas of others and asks clarifying questions

Objective

Students learn manners and language etiquette.

Materials

- We Speak Politely anchor chart (Lesson 5, p. 46)
- markers

Planning

A thinking device is an effective introduction to inspire conversation leading to new thinking. It could be a video clip, unique object (antique item, odd food), or excerpt from a book or poem that grabs the students' attention and promotes discussion and conversation.

Procedure

1. **Crafting:** Explain to students how we sometimes get new thoughts as we listen to others.

2. Model how to appropriately share thoughts that were inspired by another student's thinking using appropriate phrases: "I would like to add…"; "I like what _____ said. I also think…." Add these and other ideas to the We Speak Politely anchor chart.

3. Share your thinking device with students.

4. **Composing:** Have several students demonstrate how to use the polite phrases as they talk about the thinking device.

5. **Reflection:** Ask students how it makes them feel when someone shows they are listening in this way. Add student suggestions to the We Speak Politely anchor chart.

Points to Ponder

Appropriate language must continuously be monitored and reinforced to become permanent. Find additional opportunities to practice language etiquette, such as during line-up procedures.

Review of What Readers Read

Standards

Knows familiar print in the environment

Knows that print and written symbols convey meaning and represent spoken language

Objective

Students view themselves as readers.

Materials

- chart paper
- markers
- glue or stapler
- environmental print
- books for students

Planning

Designate a spot for students to store the environmental print they brought from home (during a previous lesson). Students will help create an environmental print anchor chart for display and reference in the classroom.

Procedure

1. **Crafting:** Title a piece of chart paper *I Can Read…*.

2. Post students' samples of environmental print. (Students can continue to add to this chart. Keep it on display for future reading practice.)

3. Read the examples together as a class.

4. **Composing:** Have students practice quiet reading at their seats for 4–7 minutes.

5. **Reflection:** Ask students to share new words they discovered using call-and-response. Have students continue to call-and-respond to each other until all students who wish to have had a chance to speak. Or, have students turn-and-talk so all have a turn.

6. Continue to revisit, reinforce, and require the respectful call-and-response format during Reader's Workshop.

Points to Ponder

A literacy workstation in your classroom can be an ideal spot to display the I Can Read… anchor chart. Encourage students to add new samples to the chart on their own.

Patience and Polite Words

Standard

Knows strategies to effectively communicate in a variety of settings

Objective

Teacher reviews manners and language etiquette with students.

Materials

- We Speak Politely anchor chart (Lesson 5, p. 46)

Planning

Prepare to role-play a polite disagreement. Base the role-play around a conflict that students will understand, such as sharing materials or holding a place in line.

Procedure

1. **Crafting:** Tell students that even if we disagree with someone, we can use our words to solve problems. Explain that they may disagree with others about a book, and learning how to disagree respectfully will be an important part of reading time.

2. Model how to agree or disagree appropriately: "I disagree with Terry, because …"; "I agree with Jared, because …". Help students understand that even if they have to disagree with others' thinking, they can still respect each other as friends.

3. **Composing:** Have several students demonstrate how to agree or disagree using appropriate language.

4. **Reflection:** Ask students if it is easy or difficult to disagree with someone. Have several students share an experience when they disagreed with a friend. Ask them what happened, and then discuss whether these tools would help make it easier to disagree.

Points to Ponder

Model this lesson with an assistant or co-teacher rather than a student. Being able to disagree in a civil manner is difficult and students may need reminders or retraining throughout the year.

I Can Read...

Standards

Knows familiar print in their environment

Knows that print and written symbols convey meaning and represent spoken language

Objective

Students practice reading environmental print and view themselves as readers.

Materials

- I Can Read... anchor chart (Lesson 7, p. 53)
- book baskets

Planning

Prepare for students to choose partners or assign them by writing students' names on craft sticks and drawing them from a cup. Make individual copies of the anchor charts for students to keep.

Procedure

1. **Crafting:** Using call-and-response, ask students to read examples of environmental print from the I Can Read... anchor chart.

2. Distribute one copy of the chart to each student. Allow students to add more examples to their own charts. Have volunteers share something they added.

3. Model reading from the I Can Read... anchor charts with a partner using respectful language.

4. **Composing:** Have students work with partners and have pairs work together in small groups to read their charts again.

5. Have students read quietly from their book baskets for 4–7 minutes.

6. **Reflection:** Ask students to reflect on interesting words they found in their reading. Use call-and-response with a few students.

Points to Ponder

Collect or have students save the mini I Can Read... charts to put in their Book Boxes for a follow-up lesson.

How to Handle a Book Box

Standard

Knows the proper way to handle books

Objective

Students develop Book Box handling skills.

Materials

- Book Care anchor chart (Lesson 1, p. 39)
- one Book Box (for demonstration purposes)

Planning

Decide where to store Book Boxes. Develop a simple procedure for collecting and returning Book Boxes. Plan how books should be kept inside the box (spine up or laying flat) and how the boxes will be labeled. Prepare an example as a model for students.

Procedure

1. **Crafting:** Show students a Book Box. Point out how many books are inside and how they are arranged. Be sure that students see where the Book Box is kept.

2. Discuss the value of having Book Boxes (holds several books in one place, helps transport books). Model the procedures for Book Boxes, including carrying the box to the group, safe and proper ways to handle the box, and returning Book Boxes.

3. **Composing:** Ask students to demonstrate the procedures. Each student is responsible for his or her own Book Box. Choose one Book Box monitor to oversee that Book Boxes are returned and organized properly. (Rotate monitors weekly.)

4. **Reflection:** Have students add tips and ideas to the Book Care anchor chart about proper book and Book Box care.

Points to Ponder

Label boxes with students' first names during the first semester and then change over to their last names for the second semester. Make the introduction to Book Boxes more fun by gift wrapping a large box with the Book Boxes inside. Each Book Box then becomes a special gift.

#50702 —Introducing Reader's Workshop: Preparing Our Youngest Readers

Choose a Book

Standards

Knows the proper way to handle books

Uses meaning clues to aid comprehension and make predictions about content

Objective

Students understand how readers make book choices.

Materials

- chart paper
- markers
- table baskets
- books of various genres for Book Box choices
- Book Boxes

Planning

Be very intentional with book selections for modeling. Use books that have colorful, interesting covers, with bold words and images. Add plenty of books to table baskets so that there is ample variety.

Procedure

1. **Crafting:** Model how readers choose books (look at covers; notice images; choose interesting subjects or favorite authors).

2. Have students share their observations of your choices. Record their responses on a piece of chart paper titled *Choose a Book.*

3. Have students make two book choices from their table baskets and add them to their Book Boxes.

4. **Composing:** Have students read quietly for 4–7 minutes. Students return Book Boxes to the storage area. Have the Book Box monitor supervise.

5. **Reflection:** Invite students to share how they made their selections, using the Choose a Book anchor chart and the criteria modeled in the lesson.

Points to Ponder

Charts are never finished. Over time, students may have new thinking on choosing books to add to the chart.

Work with Book Boxes

Standard

Exhibits care for personal belongings and school materials

Objective

Students develop organization skills for keeping Book Boxes neat and tidy.

Materials

- messy backpack
- chart paper
- markers
- Book Boxes

Planning

Determine your expectations for keeping Book Boxes organized, including arrangement of books and storage.

Procedure

1. **Crafting:** Show students an unorganized backpack containing torn papers and trash. Ask students if this is a safe place to store something important or breakable. Ask students what could be different.

2. Connect this thinking to the need for an organized Book Box. Have students set the criteria (free of trash, spines facing out) and write their ideas on chart paper.

3. **Composing:** Ask students to reorganize their Book Boxes to meet the new criteria.

4. Introduce the Book Box fairy, a secret inspector (the teacher) who makes sure the Book Box is organized properly and who may even leave a prize for an organized Book Box.

5. **Reflection:** Ask students to check their Book Boxes and determine if the Book Box fairy will likely leave a prize in their box. Ask them why or why not.

Points to Ponder

Give special reading tools, such as bookmarks, reading resource tools, or other reading-related items as rewards from the Book Box fairy. See Appendix B (pp. 160–163) for sample reward ideas.

Book Box Choices

Standards

Knows that books have titles, authors, and often illustrators

Understands that illustrations and pictures convey meaning

Objective

Students practice how to choose a book to add to their own Book Boxes.

Materials

- Choose a Book anchor chart (Lesson 9, p. 57)
- markers
- books of various genres
- Book Boxes

Planning

Spend time reviewing the Choose a Book anchor chart. Make a table basket of books for demonstration purposes. Make sure table baskets have a variety of choices.

Procedure

1. **Crafting:** Conduct a think-aloud about ways to choose books. Use the demonstration basket to show how you choose a book and your thought process as you decide if you want to add it to your Book Box.

2. Add any new criteria to the Choose a Book anchor chart. Invite students to add new criteria, as well.

3. Ask students to practice making two book choices from their table baskets and add the books to their Book Boxes. Ask students if anyone used different criteria that they would like to add to the Choose a Book anchor chart.

4. **Composing:** Have students read quietly for 5–8 minutes. Have students return Book Boxes to the storage area.

5. **Reflection:** Have three to five students describe how they made their book choices today.

Points to Ponder

If two students want to read the same book at the same time, show them how to start a book waiting list. After finishing a book, students check the waiting list and give the book to the next person listed.

Planning Calendar

	Lesson 11	Lesson 12	Lesson 13
Part 1	**Reading Rubric: Guidelines for Behavior** Learn classroom expectations for independent reading **Materials** Reading Rubric anchor chart	**Reading Expectations** Establish independent reading expectations for students **Materials** Reading Rubric chart; mini Reading Rubrics for students	**Tool Kit Introduction** Learn about Reading Tool Kits **Materials** empty tool kits; bookmarks; art supplies
Part 2	**More Ways to Choose a Book** Practice how to choose a book for Book Boxes **Materials** Choose a Book anchor chart; Reading Rubric chart; markers; books; Book Boxes	**Conferring Notebooks** Practice how to choose a book **Materials** Choose a Book anchor chart; markers; books; Book Boxes; teacher's conferring notebook	**Fiction and Nonfiction** Identify fiction and nonfiction text features **Materials** one fiction and nonfiction book on similar topics; Book Boxes; teacher's conferring notebook
Preparation	**Book selections:** **Notes:**	**Book selections:** **Notes:**	**Book selections:** **Notes:**

Planning Calendar

Lesson 14	Lesson 15	Reflection
Silent Signals Establish silent management signals and nonverbal prompts	**Turn-and-Talk** Establish turn-and-talk expectations	**What went well?** _____ _____ _____ _____ _____ _____ _____ _____ _____ _____ _____
Materials a favorite children's book	**Materials** We Speak Politely anchor chart; chart paper; markers; fiction and nonfiction books	
Characteristics of Fiction and Nonfiction Identify more characteristics of fiction and nonfiction text	**Fiction and Nonfiction Text Features** Create fiction and nonfiction genre baskets	
Materials books (fiction/nonfiction); chart paper; markers; Book Boxes; teacher's conferring notebook	**Materials** books; Fiction and Nonfiction anchor chart; cards; baskets; teacher's conferring notebook	**Areas for improvement:** _____ _____ _____
Book selections:	**Book selections:**	_____ _____ _____ _____
Notes:	**Notes:**	_____ _____ _____ _____ _____

Reading Rubric: Guidelines for Behavior

Standard

Demonstrates appropriate behaviors for relating well with others

Objective

Students learn the classroom expectations for independent reading.

Materials

- Reading Rubric chart (Appendix B, p. 153)

Planning

Plan exaggerated examples of appropriate and inappropriate behavior for each rubric level.

Procedure

1. **Crafting:** Explain to students that it is important for everyone to use appropriate reading behavior. Display the Reading Rubric chart. Discuss the expectations for each rubric level, and ask students to demonstrate examples of appropriate and inappropriate behavior for each level.

2. **Composing:** Have student volunteers demonstrate appropriate and inappropriate behaviors from the Reading Rubric chart.

3. Display the Reading Rubric chart in a place where it will be accessible and visible to students.

4. **Reflection:** Ask students how they can help themselves remember to use the Reading Rubric. How can they self-correct if they need to?

Points to Ponder

Take pictures of students that you "catch" exhibiting appropriate reading behaviors and post them or display with a banner congratulating them for being such thoughtful readers.

More Ways to Choose a Book

Standards

Knows that books have titles, authors, and often illustrators

Exhibits care for personal belongings and school materials

Objective

Students practice how to choose a book for their Book Boxes.

Materials

- Choose a Book anchor chart (Lesson 9, p. 57)
- Reading Rubric chart
- markers
- books
- Book Boxes

Planning

Choose a time when you want to review the reading rubric skills for quiet reading. The goal is not to embarrass students, but to help them practice and to reinforce appropriate behaviors.

Procedure

1. **Crafting:** Remind students about all the ways they already know how to choose a book. Refer to the Choose a Book anchor chart. Ask students if they can think of other ways to choose books (e.g., read the back cover, recognize the title from having seen the movie).

2. Ask students for suggestions to add to the Choose a Book anchor chart.

3. **Composing:** Allow 3–5 minutes for students to make two more book choices from their table baskets. Check that students now have six selections in their Book Boxes.

4. Have students read quietly for 5–8 minutes. Remind them to follow the Reading Rubric guidelines.

5. **Reflection:** Have three to five students share examples of how they made their book choices.

Points to Ponder

During independent reading, start moving around the room and have brief discussions or conferences with the students concerning book selections. Look for potential candidates for the Reflection sessions, and note who appears to be struggling.

Reading Expectations

Standards

Understands rules and the purposes they serve

Demonstrates appropriate behaviors for relating well with others

Objective

Teacher establishes independent reading expectations for students.

Materials

- Reading Rubric chart (Lesson 11, p. 62)
- mini Reading Rubrics for students (Appendix B, p. 154)
- Book Boxes

Planning

Have mini Reading Rubrics prepared to give to students to remind them about appropriate reading behaviors. These will be used as students' personal reminders.

Procedure

1. **Crafting:** Give each student a mini Reading Rubric. Read aloud the expectations on the rubric and ask students to help explain each expectation. Ask students if the information matches the Reading Rubric chart displayed in the classroom.

2. **Composing:** Ask students to role-play various reading behaviors, using mini Reading Rubrics to identify the levels (Super Stars, Shining Stars, Twinkling Stars, or Reaching for the Stars). Ask students what could have been done differently to move up a level.

3. Have students store the mini Reading Rubric in their Book Boxes so they can reflect on and evaluate their reading behaviors.

4. **Reflection:** Have students share how being a Super Star Reader will help them and other become thoughtful readers.

Points to Ponder

The rubrics will be more durable if they are printed on card stock and laminated.

Conferring Notebooks

Standards

Knows that books have titles, authors, and often illustrators

Uses emergent reading skills to "read" a story

Objective

Students practice how to choose a book, adding new skills to their repertoire.

Materials

- Choose a Book anchor chart (Lesson 9, p. 57)
- markers
- books
- Book Boxes
- teacher's conferring notebook

Planning

Have your conferring notebook prepared (see Lesson Components, pp. 28–29, for detailed information on conferring, and use the templates in Appendix B, pp. 145–146, to assemble your notebook). Plan with whom you will be conferring.

Procedure

1. **Crafting:** Tell students they will think about more ways to choose books.

2. Display the Choose a Book anchor chart. Ask students to add any new ideas about choosing a book.

3. Allow students to look at each of the books in their Book Boxes and share how they chose each book.

4. **Composing:** Students make new book choices from their table baskets and add them to their Book Boxes.

5. Have students read quietly for 5–8 minutes. During this time, confer with students about their selections. Record your notes in your conferring notebook.

6. **Reflection:** Ask three to five students to share examples of how they made their book choices.

Points to Ponder

Establish a routine and schedule for replacing student books in the Book Boxes.

Tool Kit Introduction

Standards

Understands rules and the purposes they serve

Exhibits care for personal belongings and school materials

Objective

Students learn about Reading Tool Kits.

Materials

- empty Tool Kits (pencil pouches or sealed plastic bags)
- bookmarks
- art supplies (stickers, markers, hole-punches)

Planning

Prepare bookmarks by cutting strips of colored card stock. Provide art supplies for each table so students can decorate their bookmarks.

Procedure

1. **Crafting:** Tell students that while reading today, they will determine if the books in their boxes are fiction or nonfiction. Introduce students to the Reading Tool Kits, and tell them these will be kept in the Book Boxes.

2. Show students a blank bookmark. Ask students to brainstorm some uses of a bookmark (e.g., hold your place, help you track text).

3. **Composing:** Give students blank bookmarks and tell them to use the art supplies to decorate them. Have each student write his or her name on the bookmark.

4. After students have completed their bookmarks, instruct students to keep them in their Tool Kits.

5. **Reflection:** Ask several students to share how they plan to use their bookmarks during reading.

Points to Ponder

When decorating bookmarks, use colored pencils or markers rather than crayons to avoid any wax transferring to your books. Also, avoid glitter and glue. Laminate the bookmarks for durability.

Fiction and Nonfiction

Standards

Knows the difference between fact and fiction, real and make-believe

Understands that illustrations and pictures convey meaning

Uses meaning clues to aid comprehension and make predictions about content

Objective

Students identify fiction and nonfiction text features.

Materials

- one fiction and one nonfiction book on similar topics
- Book Boxes
- teacher's conferring notebook

Planning

Choose books on similar topics but with features that clearly distinguish them as fiction or nonfiction.

Procedure

1. **Crafting:** Show students the fiction and nonfiction books. Discuss the features of the covers (cartoon drawings versus photos).

2. Read a passage from each book and ask students to compare the two again. Guide students to see that one is make-believe and the other is real. Identify these genres as fiction and nonfiction.

3. Tell students that they are to determine if the books in their boxes are fiction or nonfiction.

4. **Composing:** Have students read quietly for 5–8 minutes. Confer with individual students. See if they can distinguish between fiction and nonfiction.

5. Record notes from student conferences in your conferring notebook.

6. **Reflection:** Ask three to five students to explain how they determined whether their books were fiction or nonfiction.

Points to Ponder

Now that your lessons are becoming more centered on reading practice, give students reading goals. From this point on, you should be conferring regularly with students during their independent reading time.

Silent Signals

Standard

Understands rules and the purposes they serve

Objective

Teacher establishes silent management signals and nonverbal prompts.

Materials

- favorite children's book

Planning

Determine what signals will be the most helpful to your classroom. You will teach those first. Decide if your students will benefit from a procedural lesson (how to come to the carpet) or a management lesson (time to put hands down).

Procedure

1. **Crafting:** Explain that signals can be used in a variety of ways besides coming to the carpet. Discuss and teach a silent management signal (e.g., how to signal when it is time to put hands down if you are reading aloud or a student is speaking).

2. **Composing:** Read a story aloud. Stop as needed to reinforce the new signal.

3. **Reflection:** Ask students how silent signals help avoid interruption of instruction.

Points to Ponder

Nonverbal communication is invaluable to set and maintain the tone of Reader's Workshop. Use these vital management tools consistently.

Characteristics of Fiction and Nonfiction

Standards

Knows the difference between fact and fiction, real and make-believe

Understands that illustrations and pictures convey meaning

Uses meaning clues to aid comprehension and make predictions about content

Objective

Students identify more characteristics of fiction and nonfiction text.

Materials

- books (fiction/nonfiction)
- chart paper
- markers
- Book Boxes
- teacher's conferring notebook
- markers *(optional)*

Planning

Choose books that have enough similarities and differences to make comparisons fairly easy to find.

Procedure

1. **Crafting:** Tell students that text features help distinguish nonfiction from fiction books (e.g., factual stories based on real life versus stories in unrealistic settings with unrealistic characters, such as animals who wear clothes).

2. Read aloud and ask students if the book is fiction or nonfiction. Write *Fiction and Nonfiction* on a chart and draw two columns, labeled *Fiction is…* and *Nonfiction is…,* to record students' observations.

3. **Composing:** Have students read quietly for 5–8 minutes. Ask them to try to identify the text features that help them know if their book is fiction or nonfiction. Confer with individual students to check their understanding.

4. **Reflection:** Ask three to five students to explain how they knew their books were fiction or nonfiction and to share their evidence.

Points to Ponder

Most young readers will need help verbalizing what they are learning and how the knowledge helps them as readers. Help them find the words to express their understanding.

Turn-and-Talk

Standard

Uses language to communicate thoughts, feelings, and needs

Objective

Teacher establishes turn-and-talk expectations.

Materials

- We Speak Politely anchor chart (Lesson 5, p. 46)
- chart paper
- markers
- fiction and nonfiction books

Planning

Take note of any areas in which students may need more practice from the We Speak Politely anchor chart (Lesson 5) and review respectful etiquette.

Procedure

1. **Crafting:** Tell students they will learn how to talk about their reading with partners with a procedure called Turn-and-Talk. Ask two students to help demonstrate. Have students sit facing each other and prompt a discussion.

2. Title a sheet of chart paper *Turn-and-Talk*. Ask students what they observed and what will make turn-and-talk successful (one person talks at a time, waiting until the first speaker finishes before speaking). Chart their responses.

3. **Composing:** Have students practice turn-and-talk with partners to classify books as fiction or nonfiction.

4. **Reflection:** Ask students if their partners were good active listeners, and how they could tell. Use the call-and-response format for partners to compliment each other.

Points to Ponder

Encourage your class to use the appropriate language from previous lessons. Of course, students will learn best from your example.

Fiction and Nonfiction Text Features

Standard

Knows the difference between fact and fiction, real and make-believe

Objective

Students work together to create fiction and nonfiction genre baskets.

Materials

- books
- Fiction and Nonfiction anchor chart (Lesson 14, p. 69)
- card stock
- baskets
- teacher's conferring notebook

Planning

Make sure your class library books include fiction and nonfiction titles. Create enough fiction and nonfiction cards for every table group. Use card stock and laminate for durability.

Procedure

1. **Crafting:** Model classifying books into fiction and nonfiction categories. Use card stock to create cards labeled *Fiction* and *Nonfiction*, and point out the specific text features that help determine how to sort the books.

2. Display the Fiction and Nonfiction anchor chart.

3. **Composing:** Have students work with partners to sort the class library books, referring to the Fiction and Nonfiction chart.

4. Have partners continue to sort books for the classroom library. Confer with pairs using your teacher's conferring notebook.

5. **Reflection:** Ask students how they made their choices. Provide more books to classify as necessary.

Points to Ponder

Use the *Fiction* and *Nonfiction* sorting cards as temporary basket labels. Your session to sort the books can last as long as needed or is effective. Students may return to the task throughout the day or you may need to revisit this lesson several days in a row.

Planning Calendar

	Lesson 16	Lesson 17	Lesson 18
Part 1	**Practice Turn-and-Talk** Use turn-and-talk while identifying fiction and nonfiction **Materials** Turn-and-Talk anchor chart; Fiction and Nonfiction anchor chart; books (fiction/nonfiction)	**Mini Field Trip** Observe other students reading independently using Reading Zones **Materials** Reading Rubric chart; mini Reading Rubrics	**Reading Zones** Introduce Reading Zones in the classroom **Materials** large map of room showing Reading Zones; Reading Zone icons placed around the room
Part 2	**Read and Read Again** Understand that there is value in rereading **Materials** Three Ways to Read anchor chart; children's book; teacher's conferring notebook	**Read Books in Different Ways** Learn to reread books to gain additional information **Materials** Three Ways to Read anchor chart; children's story; teacher's conferring notebook	**Use Reading Fingers for Tracking** Introduce how to use a reading finger to track words **Materials** text displayed in large format; Book Boxes; teacher's conferring notebook
Preparation	Book selections: Notes:	Book selections: Notes:	Book selections: Notes:

Planning Calendar

Lesson 19	Lesson 20	Reflection
Reading Zone Procedures Expands Reading Zone procedures and expectations for students	**Review Silent Signals** Establish silent signals and nonverbal prompts	**What went well?** _____ _____ _____ _____ _____ _____ _____
Materials map of Reading Zones; Reading Zone icons; mini Reading Rubrics; Book Boxes; chart paper	**Materials** a favorite children's book	
Practice Tracking Track print using one-to-one correspondence	**One-to-One Correspondence** Practice tracking print using one-to-one correspondence	_____ _____ _____
Materials text (displayed, and copies for students); Book Boxes; teacher's conferring notebook	**Materials** Text (displayed, and copies for students); Book Boxes; teacher's conferring notebook	**Areas for improvement:** _____ _____ _____
Book selections:	**Book selections:**	_____ _____ _____ _____ _____
Notes:	**Notes:**	_____ _____ _____ _____

Practice Turn-and-Talk

Standards

Knows the difference between fact and fiction, real and make-believe

Uses meaning clues to aid comprehension and make predictions about content

Objective

Students use turn-and-talk while identifying fiction and nonfiction.

Materials

- Turn-and-Talk anchor chart (Lesson 15, p. 70)
- Fiction and Nonfiction anchor chart (Lesson 14, p. 69)
- books (fiction/nonfiction)

Planning

Choose a few fiction and nonfiction books. To help students identify books by the content—and not the pictures—conceal the covers.

Procedure

1. **Crafting:** Tell students they will practice distinguishing fiction from nonfiction books using turn-and-talk. Review the Turn-and-Talk anchor chart and the Fiction and Nonfiction anchor chart. Remind students of the features they used to distinguish and sort the Fiction and Nonfiction book baskets from the classroom library.

2. Read two or three pages from a book. Ask students to decide whether the book is fiction or nonfiction and to support their thinking with text evidence. Once all students agree on the genre, add the book to the proper genre basket.

3. **Composing:** Continue to share reading samples of fiction and nonfiction books. Have students turn and talk after each passage is read aloud to determine if the book shared is fiction or nonfiction.

4. **Reflection:** Have students share how they determined the genres. Add any new ideas to the Fiction and Nonfiction anchor chart.

Points to Ponder

In first and second grades, as students are more sophisticated, use nonfiction books that do not have obvious features, such as illustrations versus photos.

Read and Read Again

Standards

Uses emergent reading skills to "read" a story

Understands that illustrations and pictures convey meaning

Objective

Students understand that there is value in rereading.

Materials

- Three Ways to Read anchor chart (Lesson 3, p. 43)
- children's book
- Book Boxes
- teacher's conferring notebook

Planning

If necessary, review the Reading Rubric chart with students.

Procedure

1. **Crafting:** Tell students that thoughtful readers read something more than once. Display the Three Ways to Read anchor chart, and model reading a familiar story. Use the pictures to help retell the story. Emphasize new information that becomes apparent through reading the story a second or third time.

2. Tell students that they will read a book they have already read, but in a different way. They may use the chart to remind them of different ways to read.

3. **Composing:** Ask students to read independently for 5–8 minutes. During this time, perform a Reading Rubric check. Ask students how well they are able to follow the Reading Rubric chart.

4. Record your notes in your teacher conferring notebook as you confer with individual students.

5. **Reflection:** After quiet reading, have some students share what they learned by rereading their books.

Points to Ponder

While you are conferring, teach your students how to use a strategy or skill that will make them better readers. Have them share this information (if you decide it is appropriate) with the whole class.

Mini Field Trip

Standard

Demonstrates appropriate behaviors for relating well with others

Objective

Students observe other students reading independently, using Reading Zones.

Materials

- Reading Rubric chart (Lesson 11, p. 62)
- mini Reading Rubrics *(optional)*
- note paper *(optional)*

Planning

Make arrangements for your classroom to visit another classroom, where students are successfully using independent Reading Zones.

Procedure

1. **Crafting:** Tell students that they will be visiting another class where independent reading is happening, and they will be asked what they notice about that room.

2. Review the Reading Rubric chart. Have students look for evidence of those behaviors in the other class.

3. Review manners and etiquette, and remind students to be quiet and respectful during their visit. Visit a classroom where children are involved in independent reading time. Students may bring note paper to record what they see or they may each bring a copy of the mini Reading Rubric.

4. **Composing:** Students should notice how this class is actively engaged during independent reading time.

5. **Reflection:** After the visit, ask students to share what they observed and which behaviors contributed to a quiet and respectful room environment.

Points to Ponder

If you feel your building does not have a strong example of Reading Zones in action, there are many video clips and resources on the Internet.

#50702 – Introducing Reader's Workshop: Preparing Our Youngest Readers

Read Books in Different Ways

Standard

Relates new information to prior knowledge and experiences

Objective

Students learn to reread books to gain additional information.

Materials

- Three Ways to Read anchor chart (Lesson 3, p. 43)
- children's story
- Book Boxes
- teacher's conferring notebook

Planning

Choose a children's book as a model and plan ahead what to say for the think-aloud. Include fresh insights demonstrating the importance of reading a book more than once.

Procedure

1. **Crafting:** Read a familiar story to students. Think aloud, sharing new information gained as you reread. Point out how this adds to our understanding of a book. Exaggerate the process so it is obvious to students.

2. Tell students to read a familiar book a second time to gain new information. Display the Three Ways to Read a Book chart for reference during independent reading.

3. **Composing:** Have students read independently for 5–8 minutes. Confer with individual students and record your observations.

4. **Reflection:** Ask three to five students to share what they have learned about the story or about themselves as readers by rereading their books.

Points to Ponder

For young readers it may be necessary to provide language scaffolds for successful communication until that language becomes routine.

Reading Zones

Standard

Demonstrates appropriate behaviors for relating well with others

Objective

Teacher introduces Reading Zones in the classroom.

Materials

- large map of the room showing Reading Zones (see Appendix A, p. 135)
- teacher-created Reading Zone icons placed around the room

Planning

Map out your Reading Zones in areas that allow flexibility, comfort, and space. Use bean bag chairs, pillows, or stuffed animals to help students feel cozy. Use icons to clearly indicate Reading Zones. *Note*: Assign students to Reading Zones to spread out any possible behavior problems throughout the classroom.

Procedure

1. **Crafting:** Tell students that they will begin using Reading Zones during independent reading time.

2. Show students the Reading Zone map and introduce the icons.

3. **Composing:** Assign students to their new Reading Zone.

4. Help students locate their zones on the map and in the classroom. Practice going to Reading Zones from the Meeting Spot quickly and quietly. Dismiss students a few at a time. (This may take a few tries.)

5. **Reflection:** Ask students what helped them remember the locations of the different zones.

Points to Ponder

Try using icons for Reading Zones that are curriculum related (such as geometric shapes, animals, or sight words).

#50702 –*Introducing Reader's Workshop: Preparing Our Youngest Readers*

Use Reading Fingers for Tracking

Standard

Knows that print is read from left to right

Objective

Teacher introduces how to use a reading finger to track words.

Materials

- text displayed in large format
- Book Boxes
- teacher's conferring notebook

Planning

Think of different ways to display text in a large format (e.g., an interactive whiteboard, using a document camera, overhead projector, or commercial or crafted big book). Be sure all students can see the text.

Procedure

1. **Crafting:** Read the displayed text, and model sliding your reading finger under each word as you read it.

2. Guide students to notice that sentences consist of words flowing from left to right and top to bottom.

3. Tell students that during independent reading, they will use their reading fingers to track the words.

4. **Composing:** Have students read independently from their Book Boxes for 5–8 minutes.

5. Confer with individual students while they are reading quietly. Ask students to revisit their Reading Rubrics and self-evaluate their reading behavior.

6. **Reflection:** Ask several students to demonstrate tracking using the displayed text and tell how tracking helps them.

Points to Ponder

Consider using tracking tools to differentiate for learning styles, such as bookmarks, highlighter strips or rulers, rubber fingers that slide onto students' fingers, decorated craft sticks, or pointers.

Reading Zone Procedures

Standard

Demonstrates appropriate behaviors for relating well with others

Objective

Teacher expands Reading Zone procedures and expectations for students.

Materials

- map of Reading Zones
- Reading Zone icons
- mini Reading Rubrics
- Book Boxes
- Reading Rubric chart (*optional*) Lesson 11, p. 62)
- chart paper (*optional*)

Planning

Make a plan for how students bring Book Boxes to and from Reading Zones. Having a plan will help minimize confusion.

Procedure

1. **Crafting:** Tell students they need procedures for bringing Book Boxes to and from Reading Zones. Remind students about book care and ask them to suggest and demonstrate appropriate ways to transport books.

2. Discuss procedures with the class. If necessary, create a chart to record the procedures.

3. Have students practice. Ask one or two students to model the procedure for the rest of the class. Have students practice.

4. **Composing:** Have students read quietly in Reading Zones for 6–9 minutes.

5. **Reflection:** Revisit the Reading Rubric chart, as necessary, and ask students how well they are following their rubrics.

Points to Ponder

Since Reading Zones encompass many seating styles (e.g., chairs, floor, bean bags, or comfy nooks), think about where to place Book Boxes so that they are accessible and out of harm's way.

Practice Tracking

Standard

Knows that print is read from left to right

Objective

Students track print using one-to-one correspondence.

Materials

- text displayed in large format
- copies for students
- Book Boxes
- teacher's conferring notebook

Planning

Prepare copies of text for students to match the text you plan to present.

Procedure

1. **Crafting:** Display a passage in a large format. Model tracking print with a reading finger, reading slowly, and tracking each word as it is read.

2. Have students practice tracking along with you, using their fingers on the matching text.

3. Discuss how tracking with fingers helps us in our reading (focusing, remembering to read left to right, keeping our place).

4. Tell students that during quiet reading, they will use their reading fingers to track the text.

5. **Composing:** Have students read independently from their Book Boxes for 6–9 minutes. During this time, ask individual students to show you how they tracked. Record observations in your conferring notebook.

6. **Reflection:** Have several students show how tracking with their fingers helped them. Ask several other students how well they followed their mini Reading Rubrics.

Points to Ponder

When tracking reading, slide your finger rather than hopping. It provides a smoother transition with fluency. If you reread a word, bring your finger back to that word and continue tracking.

Review Silent Signals

Standards

Understands rules and the purposes they serve

Follows one- and two-step directions

Objective

Teacher establishes silent signals and nonverbal prompts.

Materials

- a favorite children's book

Planning

A set of silent signals was taught in Lesson 14 (p. 68). In this lesson, decide what additional signals would be valuable to the class. Keep signals simple and avoid using signals that are too similar.

Procedure

1. **Crafting:** Review the silent signals that students already know. Discuss how using silent signals helps your class run smoothly.

2. Role-play with students how classroom management might be different without silent signals.

3. Introduce new signals. Students might use signals to indicate that they have a question or a comment, or that they would like to make a prediction. Use signals to indicate that the noise level is too high or that the students should stop at a particular place in the reading to practice turn-and-talk.

4. **Composing:** Practice utilizing the new signals while reading a favorite story.

5. **Reflection:** Ask students to share ideas for new signals. Have them brainstorm different ways to help remind each other about the new signals.

Points to Ponder

Think about signals that reach beyond regular classroom management which will add specific structure to Reader's Workshop. Consider transferring your silent signals into other curriculum areas.

#50702 –Introducing Reader's Workshop: Preparing Our Youngest Readers

One-to-One Correspondence

Standard

Knows that print is read from left to right

Objective

Students practice tracking print using one-to-one correspondence.

Materials

- text displayed in large format
- copies of text for students
- Book Boxes
- teacher's conferring notebook

Planning

Choose a familiar text so students can predict the words. Provide pointers or bookmarks as students try tracking on their own.

Procedure

1. **Crafting:** Review how the reading finger helps us with reading. Display a large text sample (using a big book or an interactive whiteboard). Read the text and track with your finger. Have students practice tracking in their matching texts as you choral read. Ask students volunteers to use a pointer to track the large displayed text while the other students choral-read the words.

2. Ask students to use their reading fingers to track as they are reading today.

3. **Composing:** Have students read independently from their Book Boxes for 6–9 minutes.

4. Confer with students during independent reading time. Record your notes in your conferring notebook.

5. **Reflection:** Have several students share with the class how tracking with their finger helped them with their reading. Ask student volunteers to use a pointer to track the large displayed text while the other students choral-read the words.

Points to Ponder

Though using a tracking tool is valuable in the initial stages of reading, as soon as students are ready, help them transition to visual tracking.

Planning Calendar

	Lesson 21	Lesson 22	Lesson 23
Part 1	**Identify Book Categories** Identify book categories for the classroom library **Materials** 20–30 books from fiction baskets; card stock	**More Book Categories** Identify book categories for the classroom library **Materials** fiction books; card stock; markers	**How to Sort Books** Identify book categories for the classroom library **Materials** fiction books; card stock; markers
Part 2	**Elements of a Story: Characters** Identify characters in a story **Materials** story with strong characters; chart paper; Book Boxes; teacher's conferring notebooks	**Main Versus Supporting Characters** Practice identifying characters in a story **Materials** children's book; chart paper; sticky notes; Book Boxes; teacher's conferring notebook	**Elements of a Story: Characters in a Setting** Notice how characters and setting work together to build a story **Materials** Setting Picture Cards; Book Boxes; teacher's conferring notebook
Preparation	**Book selections:** **Notes:**	**Book selections:** **Notes:**	**Book selections:** **Notes:**

Planning Calendar

Lesson 24	Lesson 25	Reflection
Ways to Buddy Read: Body Positions and How to Share Materials Introduce buddy reading protocols	**Ways to Buddy Read: Voice Volume** Expand the buddy reading protocols to address noise level	**What went well?** _____ _____ _____ _____ _____ _____ _____
Materials reading material; Buddy Reading Management System	**Materials** reading material; Buddy Reading Management System	_____ _____ _____
Elements of a Story: Setting Identify the setting in a story	**Identify the Setting** Practice identifying settings in stories	_____ _____ _____ _____
Materials children's book with clear setting; chart paper; teacher's conferring notebook	**Materials** several stories with clear settings; Book Boxes; teacher's conferring notebook	**Areas for improvement:** _____ _____ _____
Book selections:	**Book selections:**	_____ _____ _____
Notes:	**Notes:**	_____ _____ _____ _____ _____

Identify Book Categories

Standard

Knows the basic characteristics of familiar genres

Objective

Students identify book categories for the classroom library.

Materials

- 20–30 books from fiction baskets
- card stock

Planning

Choose books that reflect a few obvious categories. Announce that you are looking for a specific book (a familiar story from the classroom library), but you cannot find it. Ask students to try and find it in the library.

Procedure

1. **Crafting:** Remind students that you were trying to find a specific book. Discuss if it was easy or difficult to locate the book.

2. Show students how it would be easy to find books if they were organized by categories. Ask them for ideas about how to organize books.

3. Think aloud as you look through the books selected for the lesson. Focus on similarities among books.

4. **Composing:** Have students help you sort the books into categories and place them into baskets.

5. Label the baskets with genre codes similar to *Fiction* and *Nonfiction* and add the baskets to the library.

6. **Reflection:** Ask students if there are any pictures that they can add to the genre codes to help them remember the different categories.

Points to Ponder

With this first book sort, it is extremely important that categories are obvious (e.g., sorted by well-known characters).

Elements of a Story: Characters

Standard

Knows setting, main characters, main events, sequence, narrator, and problems in stories

Objective

Students identify characters in a story.

Materials

- story with strong characters
- chart paper
- Book Boxes
- teacher's conferring notebook

Planning

Just like a cake needs the proper ingredients, so does a good story. The ingredients in a story are called *story elements*. Prepare a chart titled *Characters* that shows character elements. Include a definition, and some examples (e.g., "a *character* is who the story is about"; "characters can be people, animals, or fantasy creatures").

Procedure

1. **Crafting:** Read a story aloud to the class. Think aloud about the characters. Discuss who they are, what they are like, and how many characters are in the story. Give evidence to explain your thoughts.

2. Encourage students to add their comments and facilitate a discussion about the characters. Record their answers on a sheet of chart paper titled Characters.

3. **Composing:** Tell students that they will practice identifying characters in their books.

4. As students read independently for 6–9 minutes, confer with individual students about how they decided who were the main characters in their stories.

5. **Reflection:** Have those students share with the class how they identified the characters in their stories.

Points to Ponder

As with any introductory lesson, key points should be perceptible to the point of obvious. Keep the anchor chart accessible so students can add ideas later.

More Book Categories

Standards

Uses reading skills and strategies to understand a variety of familiar literary text

Knows the basic characteristics of familiar genres

Objective

Students identify book categories for the class library.

Materials

- fiction books
- card stock
- markers

Planning

Make sure the books you choose reflect some obvious categories that students will be able to identify easily.

Procedure

1. **Crafting:** Ask students if there are other types of book categories they have noticed in the fiction baskets (e.g., fairy tales, science fiction, animal stories, or holiday stories.)

2. Think aloud as you sort through the books selected for the lesson. Point out common traits. Ask students if they notice other common traits.

3. **Composing:** Ask the students to help sort the books into more categories and then work together to label the categories.

4. Have students add the new genre baskets to the library.

5. **Reflection:** Ask students to explain how they picked their new genres. Ask if there are books that could fit into more than one category and how those should be sorted.

Points to Ponder

Students will feel more ownership of the library if they are allowed to create the book basket genre labels. If you are concerned about readability, write the genres yourself and have students illustrate them to reflect the category.

Main Versus Supporting Characters

Standards

Knows setting, main characters, main events, sequence, narrator, and problems in stories

Knows the main idea or theme of a story, drama, or poem

Objective

Students practice identifying characters in a story.

Materials

- children's book with strong characters
- chart paper
- sticky notes
- Book Boxes
- teacher's conferring notebook

Planning

Choose a story that has an obvious main character and supporting characters. For younger students, consider a story that only has a few supporting characters to avoid confusion.

Procedure

1. **Crafting:** Read a story aloud. Stop as each new character is introduced and ask students to identify the characters. Write the characters' names and distinguishing traits on large sticky notes.

2. Discuss the difference between main and secondary characters. On chart paper, draw two columns. Label one column *Main Character* and the other column *Supporting Characters*. Discuss with students where to place each character sticky note. Have them explain their thinking.

3. **Composing:** Students identify characters in their stories as they read quietly for 8–10 minutes. Ask individual students what helped them decide who are the main characters.

4. Students draw sketches of the characters and circle the most important ones. Students place a finger on the sketch each time that character appears.

5. **Reflection:** Have students share how they knew which characters in their book were the main ones.

Points to Ponder

Character lessons may need to be repeated or extended until you have conferred with all students about characters. This is also true with other story elements.

How to Sort Books

Standard

Knows the basic characteristics of familiar genres

Objective

Students identify book categories for the classroom library.

Materials

- fiction books
- card stock
- markers

Planning

Books still need to reflect categories, but now the categories can be more refined. Choose books that will challenge students to be creative in the categories they select.

Procedure

1. **Crafting:** Students will be creating new categories for the library. Students will need time to analyze books for common traits (characters, settings, text features). For younger students, read book titles aloud to help them gain familiarity with the stories.

2. Tell students that you want them to look over the books and find similarities. Help guide student thinking as needed.

3. **Composing:** Have students categorize the books and label the baskets using card stock and markers. Ask students to decorate the labels to help identify the categories for nonreaders. Add the new genre baskets to the library.

4. **Reflection:** Ask students to share what book categories they added and to explain their thinking

Points to Ponder

Category titles can reflect student language (e.g., "Animals who wear clothes"). Continue sorting books into obvious groups until no apparent categories remain. Prepare additional lessons on identifying book categories as needed.

Elements of a Story: Characters in a Setting

Standards

Knows setting, main characters, main events, sequence, narrator, and problems in stories

Knows the main idea or theme of a story, drama, or poem

Objective

Students notice how characters and setting work together to build a story.

Materials

- Setting Picture Cards (Appendix B, pp. 164–165)
- Book Boxes
- teacher's conferring notebook

Planning

Prepare Setting Picture Cards (or pictures from your own collection) that reflect varied, easy-to-recognize places.

Procedure

1. **Crafting:** Show students different Setting Picture Cards. Think aloud about how you determine the characteristics of each setting (e.g., the background, locations, clues that show the time of day).

2. Ask students what kinds of characters they might find in different settings (e.g., *astronauts* in a spaceship). Model how the setting helps you anticipate what kinds of characters to expect. Show explicit evidence from the cards.

3. **Composing:** Have students find main characters and notice the settings around those characters as they read independently for 8–10 minutes.

4. Ask individual students as they are reading how knowledge of the settings combined with the characters' traits gave insight into the story or impacted their understanding.

5. **Reflection:** Ask students to share how the main characters and setting fit together in their stories.

Points to Ponder

Technology such as *Microsoft PowerPoint*® slide shows, interactive whiteboards, and document cameras can permit students to easily see picture details.

Ways to Buddy Read: Body Positions and How to Share Materials

Standard

Demonstrates appropriate behaviors for relating well with others

Objective

Teacher introduces buddy reading protocols.

Materials

- reading material (book, poem, etc.)
- Buddy Reading Management System (Appendix D, pp. 168–171)

Planning

A Buddy Reading Management System (BRMS) is an organized way to match students for partner work, such as drawing craft sticks with the students' names, or more complex systems such as Cipher Wheel, Tick Tock Pals, Appointment Buddies, or Cordial Calling (see descriptions in Appendix D, pp. 168–171). Choose a management system to assign partners for buddy reading practice.

Procedure

1. **Crafting:** Tell students that buddy reading is a great way to hear the words and understand a story with a partner. Model buddy reading with a student.

2. Ask students about your body positions—were you ear to ear, shoulder to shoulder, or face to face? Which was the best way to read with a buddy?

3. Show students different ways to share the book when reading together as partners.

4. **Composing:** Use one of the management systems listed above to assign partners to students. Have students practice buddy reading for 8–10 minutes.

5. **Reflection:** Ask students to share what body positions worked best when working with partners.

Points to Ponder

Carefully consider the Buddy Reading Management System you choose. Some will be more appropriate for kindergarten students than first or second grade; others will fit better with older students. Remember, variations of all styles are possible.

Elements of a Story: Setting

Standard

Knows setting, main characters, main events, sequence, narrator, and problems in stories

Objective

Students identify the setting in a story.

Materials

- children's book with clear setting
- chart paper
- teacher's conferring notebook

Planning

Prepare an anchor chart titled *Setting,* with columns labeled *Place* (where the story happens); *Time* (when the story takes place); and *Environment* (external factors).

Procedure

1. **Crafting:** Read aloud to students. Model how you find the setting. Read only enough to identify the setting. Think aloud and name the different elements that you notice. Give evidence to explain your thoughts.

2. Ask students what other details they noticed about the setting. Record their observations on the *Setting* anchor chart.

3. **Composing:** Tell students they will practice identifying settings in their books as they read independently for 8–10 minutes. Confer with individual students during this time and record your conversations.

4. **Reflection:** Ask several students to share with the class how they identified the setting in their stories.

Points to Ponder

To challenge your readers and differentiate between grade levels, choose books where the setting changes as the story progresses.

Ways to Buddy Read: Voice Volume

Standard

Understands rules and the purposes they serve

Objective

Teacher expands the buddy reading protocol to address noise level.

Materials

- reading material
- Buddy Reading Management System (Appendix D, pp. 168–171)

Planning

For protocol practice, students should work with a consistent partner.

Procedure

1. **Crafting:** Tell students that during buddy reading, each student needs to be heard, and all students need to be respectful of the other students who are trying to hear each other. Discuss appropriate voice volume when buddy reading (quiet or whisper voice).

2. Model appropriate and inappropriate voice volumes for students. Ask them to point out how these are different.

3. **Composing:** Have several students demonstrate an appropriate volume for buddy reading.

4. Have students practice buddy reading with partners. Circulate around the room and remind students about appropriate voice volume when necessary.

5. **Reflection:** Ask students to share the polite words they used to remind each other to use appropriate volumes.

Points to Ponder

Demonstrate vocal-chord vibrations in normal speech by having students hold their hands to their throats while speaking. Show how there is no vibration when they whisper. Consider adding a silent signal as a reminder to check voice volume.

Identify the Setting

Standards

Knows setting, main characters, main events, sequence, narrator, and problems in stories

Knows the main idea or theme of a story, drama, or poem

Objective

Students practice identifying settings in stories.

Materials

- several stories with clear settings
- Book Boxes
- teacher's conferring notebook

Planning

Choose several stories with clear settings that differ. Add some interest by varying genres.

Procedure

1. **Crafting:** Read passages from several stories aloud and model how you find the setting. Think aloud what you would expect about the story or the characters based on that type of location.

2. Explain how the setting helps you better understand the story (gives you a sense of what to expect).

3. **Composing:** Tell students they will identify the setting as they read independently for 8–10 minutes. They should think about what they would expect from that setting.

4. During quiet reading, confer with individual students and ask them to point out elements of the setting and how those elements relate to the story.

5. **Reflection:** Have several students share with the class how knowing the setting helped them better understand what to expect in their stories.

Points to Ponder

Supply extensive and explicit modeling in your think-aloud about how understanding the characters and setting gives deeper meaning to the story. Students may mimic your words, but over time they will be able to use their own explanations.

Planning Calendar

	Lesson 26	Lesson 27	Lesson 28
Part 1	**Final Book Categories** Identify final book categories for the classroom library **Materials** books with no clear categories; card stock; markers	**Ways to Buddy Read: Turn Reading** Introduce turn reading **Materials** Buddy Reading Management System (BRMS); book; chart paper; markers	**Ways to Buddy Read: Echo Reading** Introduce echo reading **Materials** BRMS; Ways to Buddy Read anchor chart; markers; Book Boxes; teacher's conferring notebook
Part 2	**Purpose of a Setting** Gain a deeper understanding of the purpose of a story's setting **Materials** book to read aloud; Book Boxes; teacher's conferring notebook	**The Setting as a Problem** Understand how the setting can also be the problem within the story **Materials** book to read aloud; Book Boxes; teacher's conferring notebook	**Character and Setting Response** Practice thinking about characters and settings using pictures to give clues **Materials** Character and Setting response sheets; Book Boxes; teacher's conferring notebook
Preparation	Book selections: Notes:	Book selections: Notes:	Book selections: Notes:

Planning Calendar

Lesson 29	Lesson 30	Reflection
Ways to Buddy Read: Choral Reading Introduce choral reading	**Buddy Reading in Action** Review all three ways to buddy read	**What went well?** _____ _____ _____ _____ _____ _____ _____ _____
Materials familiar reading material; BRMS; Ways to Buddy Read anchor chart; markers	**Materials** reading material; Ways to Buddy Read anchor chart; BRMS; chart paper; markers	
Elements of a Story: Problem and Solution Introduce the story elements of problem and solution	**Elements of a Story: Characters, Setting, Problem, and Solution** Identify the problem and solution among story elements	_____ _____
Materials book to read aloud; sticky notes; Book Boxes; teacher's conferring notebook	**Materials** fiction book; story glove; Book Boxes; teacher's conferring notebook; story elements icons	**Areas for improvement:** _____ _____
Book selections:	**Book selections:**	_____ _____ _____ _____
Notes:	**Notes:**	_____ _____ _____ _____

Final Book Categories

Standards

Uses reading skills and strategies to understand a variety of familiar literary text

Knows the basic characteristics of familiar genres

Objective

Students identify final book categories for the classroom library.

Materials

- books with no clear categories
- card stock
- markers

Planning

All classroom library books that show obvious categories have been sorted, placed in labeled containers, and returned to the newly organized library. This exercise will allow students to determine categories for any remaining books.

Procedure

1. **Crafting:** Students will need additional time to peruse the remaining books before sorting. Students look for books that do not fit into any of the existing categories.

2. It is possible that some books cannot be grouped. Work with students to brainstorm solutions for sorting these titles.

3. **Composing:** Have students sort books into as many categories as possible and label the containers using markers and card stock.

4. Add the final genre baskets to the library.

5. **Reflection:** Have students share their latest book basket categories and explain the kinds of books they contain. Do a quick review of the newly categorized classroom library.

Points to Ponder

Even though this is the last time categories are formally addressed, over time students may discover new categories that need to be added, such as specific curriculum categories when new units are introduced.

Purpose of a Setting

Standards

Knows setting, main characters, main events, sequence, narrator, and problems in stories

Knows the main idea or theme of a story, drama, or poem

Objective

Students gain a deeper understanding of the purpose of a story's setting.

Materials

- book to read aloud
- Book Boxes
- teacher's conferring notebook

Planning

Find a story in which the setting creates a problem for the character, such as a storm, a locked room, or an enchanted castle.

Procedure

1. **Crafting:** Read aloud your book selection and stop when it becomes evident that the setting is contributing to the problem. Share your thinking. Make students aware of how the setting is creating problems for the main character.

2. Ask students how the story might change if the setting was different.

3. Tell students their reading goal is to notice if the setting in their book creates a problem for the character(s).

4. **Composing:** Have students read independently from their Book Boxes for 10–12 minutes. During this time, confer with individual students. Ask them how they identified the setting and whether the setting created a problem for the characters.

5. **Reflection:** Ask student volunteers to share how they decided if the setting was a problem or not.

Points to Ponder

Setting as a conflict can be a difficult concept. You will want to revisit this later in the year.

Ways to Buddy Read: Turn Reading

Standard

Demonstrates appropriate behaviors for relating well with others

Objective

Teacher introduces turn reading.

Materials

- Buddy Reading Management System (Appendix D, pp. 168–171)
- reading material
- chart paper
- markers

Planning

Learning how to take turns is an important developmental social skill. Students will need many opportunities to practice.

Procedure

1. **Crafting:** Students will learn about turn reading. In turn reading, one student reads a page or sentence, then the partner reads the next page or sentence. Demonstrate how this looks using a student volunteer.

2. **Composing:** Assign partners to students. Have partners practice this strategy for 7–9 minutes.

3. **Reflection:** Call students to the Large Group Meeting Spot. Congratulate them on successful buddy reading. On a sheet of chart paper, write *Ways to Buddy Read*. Below the title, write *1. Turn Reading*. Ask students to brainstorm ideas to make turn reading successful (wait patiently for your turn to read; do not read ahead).

Points to Ponder

No matter the grade level, students need to learn and practice how to work with partners. Buddy reading helps them to practice this valuable life skill. Have students change partners so they experience working with different students.

The Setting as a Problem

Standard

Knows setting, main characters, main events, sequence, narrator, and problems in stories

Objective

Students understand how the setting can also be the problem within the story.

Materials

- book to read aloud
- Book Boxes
- teacher's conferring notebook

Planning

Choose one or two books in which the setting is the problem. Try to find books that depict different problems. These could stem from place, time, or environmental factors.

Procedure

1. **Crafting:** Read aloud from book selections. As soon as it is revealed, stop and discuss how the setting has become the problem in the story. It is not necessary to read the entire book—the aim is to compare and contrast different settings that are problematic.

2. Tell students their reading goal will be to notice if the settings in their books cause problems for the characters.

3. **Composing:** Have students read independently from their Book Boxes for 10–12 minutes. During independent reading, confer with individual students. Have students describe how the setting is the problem in the story.

4. **Reflection:** Ask students to practice turn-and-talk to share information about the settings in their stories.

Points to Ponder

You may want to differentiate this reading goal as necessary for your grade level. Since this is a more difficult concept, revisit this reading goal throughout the year.

Ways to Buddy Read: Echo Reading

Standard

Demonstrates appropriate behaviors for relating well with others

Objective

Teacher introduces echo reading.

Materials

- Buddy Reading Management System
- Ways to Buddy Read anchor chart (Lesson 27, p. 100)
- markers
- Book Boxes
- teacher's conferring notebook

Planning

Use a familiar text, song, poem or nursery rhyme. Students should not be struggling through the text to practice buddy reading.

Procedure

1. **Crafting:** Tell students that they will learn a new way to buddy read, called *Echo Reading*. In echo reading, one student reads a page or sentence. The partner echoes by reading the exact same page or sentence.

2. Model the new strategy with another teacher or student. Remind students that they should still use their inside voices, both as the reader and as the echo. Add *Echo Reading* to the Ways to Buddy Read anchor chart.

3. **Composing:** Have students work with partners or small groups to practice echo reading.

4. **Reflection:** Have students comment on what they did to make echo reading successful. Record their ideas under *Echo Reading* on the chart.

Points to Ponder

Have students make "telephones" out of foam cups connected by a piece of string which is tied through pinholes in the base of each cup. A student reads into one cup, and another student listens through the second cup.

Character and Setting Response

Standard

Predicts story events or outcome using illustrations and prior knowledge as a guide

Objective

Students practice thinking about characters and settings using pictures to give clues.

Materials

- Character and Setting Response Sheets, and a large-format version to display (Appendix B, pp. 155–158)
- Book Boxes
- teacher's conferring notebook

Planning

Display the Character and Setting Response Sheet so that it is visible to all. Prepare individual pages, if necessary.

Procedure

1. **Crafting:** Display the Character and Setting Response Sheet. Ask students to describe the first setting (spaceship). Ask what details gave clues about this setting. Model a few examples.

2. Have students name at least three different characters they might expect to see in this setting. Write their responses on the display, while they write or draw their responses on their own pages. Complete the examples together as a class.

3. **Composing:** Tell students they will identify characters they would expect to find in the settings in their stories as they read independently for 10–12 minutes. Confer with students about characters and setting; record comments in your conferring notebook.

4. **Reflection:** Ask students how knowing the characters and the setting help them better understand the story.

Points to Ponder

If you are ready to take your students a little deeper with characters and setting, model how to step into the story to create character and setting empathy.

Ways to Buddy Read: Choral Reading

Standard

Demonstrates appropriate behaviors for relating well with others

Objective

Teacher introduces choral reading.

Materials

- familiar reading material
- Buddy Reading Management System (Appendix D, pp. 168–171)
- Ways to Buddy Read anchor chart (Lesson 27, p. 100)
- markers

Planning

Choral reading works best with very familiar text. Ideally find something the students have read before.

Procedure

1. **Crafting:** Tell students that they will learn about a way to buddy read called *Choral Reading*. In choral reading, partners read the same selection of the same book at the same time.

2. Ask a student volunteer or another teacher to model the strategy with you. Have a few students demonstrate choral reading for the class. Add *Choral Reading* to the Ways to Buddy Read anchor chart.

3. **Composing:** Have students work with partners or small groups to practice choral reading.

4. **Reflection:** Have students comment on what they did to make choral reading successful (stay in sync, each student reads at the same volume, students use the same inflections). Record their ideas under *Choral Reading* on the anchor chart.

Points to Ponder

Reinforce polite words and social etiquette. Move about the room and listen to partners as they interact to reinforce appropriate behaviors.

Elements of a Story: Problem and Solution

Standards

Knows the main idea or theme of a story, drama, or poem

Knows setting, main characters, main events, sequence, narrator, and problems in stories

Objective

Teacher introduces the story elements of problem and solution.

Materials

- a book to read aloud that has an obvious problem and solution (also displayed in a large format)
- sticky notes
- Book Boxes
- teacher's conferring notebook

Planning

Since problem and solution are not quite as obvious in some texts, the teacher may want to prepare a basket of carefully preselected books that will allow students to achieve their reading goals. This is especially important with younger readers.

Procedure

1. **Crafting:** Almost all stories have a problem that needs to be solved. Explain that problems are usually introduced at the beginning of a story (the rest of the story is about solving this problem).

2. Display a passage from a familiar story. Think aloud to show how you identify a problem and discover the solution. Use sticky notes to mark your thinking.

3. **Composing:** Tell students to try to locate the problem and solutions in their own stories as they read independently for 10–12 minutes.

4. **Reflection:** During this time, ask students how they found the problem and how they could identify a solution. Record observations in your conferring notebook. Ask the same students to share how they discovered the problem and solution in their books.

Points to Ponder

Since problems exist in nearly all fiction stories, the ability to find and understand them is essential. Depending upon grade level, consider expanding the number of lessons about problem and solution and revisiting them during the year.

Buddy Reading in Action

Standard

Demonstrates appropriate behaviors for relating well with others

Objective

Students review all three ways to buddy read.

Materials

- reading material
- Ways to Buddy Read anchor chart (Lesson 27, p. 100)
- Buddy Reading Management System (Appendix D, pp. 168–171)
- chart paper
- markers

Planning

Decide if and how often you want students to change reading buddies. Share your decision with students. Plan out a specific amount of time to play the Ready, Set, Buddy Read! game.

Procedure

1. **Crafting:** Display the Ways to Buddy Read anchor chart. Have student volunteers model the three ways to buddy read. On a new sheet of chart paper, draw a two-column T-chart. Label the first column *Looks Like…,* and the second column *Sounds Like…,* and title the chart *Looks Like, Sounds Like.* Ask students what buddy reading looks like and sounds like. Record their answers in the appropriate columns.

2. Have students work with partners to demonstrate the ways to buddy read.

3. **Composing:** Play Ready, Set, Buddy Read! Partners select one way to buddy read. Set the timer and announce, "Ready, set, buddy read!" When the timer sounds, reset it and have partners choose another way to read. Continue play for several rounds.

4. **Reflection:** Ask students which way worked best for them, which way was most difficult, and why.

Points to Ponder

Try using a visual timer to help students gauge the amount of time that elapsed.

Elements of a Story: Characters, Setting, Problem, and Solution

Standard

Knows setting, main characters, main events, sequence, narrator, and problems in stories

Objective

Students identify the problem and solution among story elements.

Materials

- short fiction book
- story glove
- Book Boxes
- teacher's conferring notebook
- story elements icons (Teacher Resource CD) *(optional)*

Planning

Prepare a story glove using a cloth garden glove. There are two ways to use the glove: Write story elements on each finger and thumb (thumb—characters; pointer finger—setting; middle finger—problem; ring finger—solution; pinky—moral or lesson). Or, glue a symbol that represents each of the five story elements onto each finger. (Sample icons are available on the Teacher Resource CD.)

Procedure

1. **Crafting:** Think aloud about the characters, setting, problem, and solution as you read a story. Point out any moral or lesson found. Use the story elements icons while reading to aid the students' understanding.

2. Retell the story with the story glove. Point to each finger as you discuss that story element.

3. **Composing:** Have students look for problems and solutions in stories as they read independently for 12–15 minutes. During this time, confer with individual students.

4. Students can trace their hands on a sheet of paper and draw the story elements on the corresponding fingers to recall the story glove.

5. **Reflection:** Ask students to share a problem and solution they found in their reading.

Points to Ponder

Use picture icons that are story specific (use a pig for character, a house for setting, and so on). Think about adding story glove props to your reading area.

Planning Calendar

	Lesson 31	Lesson 32	Lesson 33
Part 1	**Buddy Reading Management System** Reinforce the Buddy Reading Management System **Materials** BRMS; ways to Buddy Read anchor chart	**Independent and Buddy Reading in Action** Combine independent and buddy reading in the same session **Materials** reading material; BRMS; Ways to Buddy Read anchor chart; bell, chime, or other noisemaker	**Use a Sticky Note to Mark Your Thinking** Introduce Tool Kits and show how to use sticky notes during reading **Materials** reading material; student and teacher's Tool Kits; sticky notes
Part 2	**Practice Identifying Story Elements** Identify story elements leading up to the moral or lesson **Materials** short fiction book; story glove; Book Boxes; teacher's conferring notebook	**Find Story Elements in Unfamiliar Text** Identify the problem, solution, and big idea in a story **Materials** an unfamiliar story; sticky notes; Book Boxes; teacher's conferring notebook	**Elements of a Story: Cause and Effect** Identify cause-and-effect relationships in a story **Materials** cause-and-effect story; sticky notes
Preparation	**Book selections:** **Notes:**	**Book selections:** **Notes:**	**Book selections:** **Notes:**

Planning Calendar

Lesson 34	Lesson 35	Reflection
Use Highlighter Tape Use highlighter tape during reading	**Replace Tool Kit Materials** Replace the reading tools	**What went well?** _____ _____ _____ _____ _____ _____ _____
Materials text (in large format); Highlighter Cards, student Tool Kits	**Materials** student Tool Kits; replacement tools	_____ _____ _____
Cause-and-Effect Response Practice identifying cause-and-effect relationships in stories	**Look for Cause-and-Effect Relationships** Identify cause and effect in a story	**Areas for improvement:** _____
Materials markers; chart paper; Cause-and-Effect Response Sheets; Ways to Buddy Read chart; text; conferring notebook	**Materials** story; chart paper; markers; Book Boxes; conferring notebook	_____ _____ _____
Book selections:	**Book selections:**	_____ _____ _____ _____
Notes:	**Notes:**	_____ _____ _____ _____

Buddy Reading Management System

Standard

Demonstrates appropriate behaviors for relating well with others

Objective

Teacher reinforces the Buddy Reading Management System.

Materials

- Buddy Reading Management System (Appendix D, pp. 168–171)
- Ways to Buddy Read anchor chart (Lesson 27, p. 100)

Planning

Decide where you want buddy pairs to read (an assigned Reading Zone, at their desks, etc.).

Procedure

1. **Crafting:** Discuss the management system's purpose and how to use it. (For example, if using the Cipher Wheel, explain that each student's name is written in a slot on either the inner or outer wheel. Turn the inner wheel to match up slots to determine partners.)

2. Ask several students to model how they find their reading buddy.

3. Point out the areas where students may choose to read together. Students will need to quickly decide where to go to read.

4. **Composing:** Practice the process until students master the buddy management rituals and routines. Students should brainstorm ways to handle conflicts.

5. Have students buddy read for 10–12 minutes.

6. **Reflection:** Ask students if they were content with their partners, and why or why not. Have students brainstorm ways to handle a conflict with a partner.

Points to Ponder

Some students may need additional practice to master finding their buddy according to the Buddy Reading Management System chosen. Allow lots of opportunities to practice.

Practice Identifying Story Elements

Standards

Knows the main idea or theme of a story, drama, or poem

Relates stories to personal experiences

Objective

Students identify story elements leading up to the moral or lesson.

Materials

- short fiction book to read aloud
- story glove (from Lesson 30, p. 107)
- Book Boxes
- teacher's conferring notebook

Planning

Your students' reading experiences will determine their ability to find the moral or lesson of the story. Look for texts that are appropriate for your students' reading level and background knowledge.

Procedure

1. **Crafting:** Tell students that stories have a moral or lesson, either about a "big idea" or about a specific behavior or character trait. Often, the author trusts the reader to figure out the moral of the story.

2. Read aloud from a fiction text. Model how you find the problem, solution and the moral or lesson. Use the story glove to retell the story elements.

3. Ask students to help you retell the story. Have them articulate different story elements.

4. **Composing:** Tell students to look for the moral in their own reading as they read independently for 12–15 minutes. Confer with students during this time, recording notes in your conferring notebook.

5. **Reflection:** Remind students how you found the big idea or lesson in your story. Ask students if anyone would like to share a big idea or lesson from a story.

Points to Ponder

If you want your story elements to be interchangeable, try using hook-and-loop dots on the story glove.

Independent and Buddy Reading in Action

Standard

Understands rules and the purposes they serve

Objective

Students combine independent and buddy reading in the same session.

Materials

- reading material
- Buddy Reading Management System (Appendix D, pp. 168–171)
- Ways to Buddy Read anchor chart (Lesson 27, p. 100)
- bell, chime, or other noisemaker

Planning

Determine an auditory signal to let students know when it is time to transition from independent to buddy reading.

Procedure

1. **Crafting:** Students will practice moving from independent reading into buddy reading using a new signal, such as a bell or a chime.

2. Have students brainstorm appropriate ways to transition into working with their buddies (move quietly, bring your book with you, no running). Practice the behaviors. Display the Ways to Buddy Read anchor chart and remind students of their options for buddy reading.

3. **Composing:** Students go to their Reading Zones for a mock independent reading. At a random time, give the auditory signal. Have students transition into buddy reading, and read for 5–7 minutes.

4. **Reflection:** Have students share how they decided where to read. How did they determine which way to buddy read?

Points to Ponder

Practice as much as necessary until a smooth transition is mastered. Buddy reading can also be viewed as a privilege or motivation for staying on task during independent reading.

Find Story Elements in Unfamiliar Text

Standard

Knows setting, main characters, main events, sequence, narrator, and problems in stories

Objective

Students will identify the problem, solution, and big idea in a story.

Materials

- large display of a story with an obvious problem and solution
- sticky notes
- Book Boxes
- teacher's conferring notebook

Planning

Read through your story selection ahead of time, identify where you will mark your thinking, and plan what you might say.

Procedure

1. **Crafting:** Tell students you are going to read to find a problem, solution, and moral or lesson in a book you have not read before. Read aloud and model thinking aloud to find the problem and solution. Use sticky notes to mark your thinking on the displayed text. Encourage students to share additional ideas.

2. After reading, discuss what the author wanted us to understand. Tell students this is the moral or lesson.

3. **Composing:** Tell students that they can use these same strategies when they read a new book.

4. Revisit the Reading Rubric chart. Have students read independently from their Book Boxes for 12–15 minutes. Confer with students during this time and record your observations.

5. **Reflection:** Ask students to share how they found a problem, solution, and a big idea or lesson in their stories.

Points to Ponder

Lead students to discover the author's purpose. Do not discount student thinking that seems off target, but use questioning techniques to probe more deeply into their thinking. Ask students where in the text they were able to determine the author's purpose.

Use a Sticky Note to Mark Your Thinking

Standard

Knows setting, main characters, main events, sequence, narrator, and problems in stories

Objective

Students are introduced to Tool Kits and shown how to use sticky notes during reading.

Materials

- reading material
- student Tool Kit
- teacher's Tool Kit (Appendix B, p. 147)
- sticky notes

Planning

Choose an old favorite for your read-aloud. Be deliberate in the use of the sticky notes. Plan your thinking so you can show the students authentic examples of how the sticky notes should be used.

Procedure

1. **Crafting:** Read aloud. Use a few sticky notes to mark your thinking about setting or characters. Tell students that they will have sticky notes in their Tool Kits. Tell students that these will be kept in their Book Boxes to hold tools that will help with reading.

2. Distribute student Tool Kits and sticky notes. Instruct students to use their sticky notes to mark a description of a character or setting.

3. **Composing:** Monitor students as they read independently for a short time, practicing using sticky notes. Have students store sticky notes in their Tool Kits and place the kits in their Book Boxes.

4. **Reflection:** Have students share how they used their sticky notes. Add more sticky notes to Tool Kits (1–5 per student).

Points to Ponder

Have students draw or describe their thinking on a sticky note, then add the page number and their initials to the bottom. Students can tape all of their sticky notes to a sheet of paper or in their Reader's Notebooks for feedback.

Elements of a Story: Cause and Effect

Standard

Uses meaning clues to aid comprehension and make predictions about content

Objective

Students identify cause-and-effect relationships in a story.

Materials

- a story that has obvious cause-and-effect situations
- sticky notes

Planning

Use an old favorite to read aloud. Have an explicit plan of where you will model your thinking in the story.

Procedure

1. **Crafting:** Tell students that cause and effect means one event causes another event to happen. The *cause* tells why it happens and the *effect* tells the result.

2. Read a story such as Laura Numeroff's *If You Give a Mouse a Cookie* (1985). Think aloud how you identify the cause and effect relationships. Ask students to predict the effects or recall the causes as you read.

3. **Composing:** Students read independently for 12–15 minutes and use their sticky notes to mark a cause or effect. Confer with students during this time and write your observations in your conferring notebook.

4. Transition to buddy reading. Have students practice buddy reading for 5–7 minutes.

5. **Reflection:** Ask students to share the causes and effects they find.

Points to Ponder

Identifying cause-and-effect relationships may be difficult. Not all books have obvious cause-and-effect formats. Use your conferring time to help students find these relationships, and then prepare them to teach others how to do it during the Reflection Session.

Use Highlighter Tape

Standard

Exhibits care for personal belongings and school materials

Objective

Students learn how to use highlighter tape during reading.

Materials

- text displayed in large format
- Highlighter Cards (Appendix C, p. 167)
- student Tool Kits

Planning

Think of ways that highlighter tape can assist your students in their learning, such as highlighting specific letters, sight words, or words they do not know. Decide what you want students to highlight in this lesson.

Procedure

1. **Crafting:** Model how to use highlighter tape by displaying a passage in large format and placing the tape over the text to highlight a letter, a high-frequency word, an unknown word, and so on.

2. Tell students they will add highlighter tape to their Tool Kits. Model taking the tape off the text and putting it back onto the Highlighter Card. Pass out Highlighter Cards with tape, and give students direction about what to highlight as they read.

3. **Composing:** Have students read independently using highlighter tape.

4. **Reflection:** Have students share words they highlighted. Monitor that all students have returned the tape to their Highlighter Cards and make sure the cards are returned to students' Tool Kits.

Points to Ponder

Highlighter tape comes in different widths, so choose a size that is appropriate for your grade level. Also, different colors of highlighter tape can be beneficial to visual learners or to students with reading challenges.

Cause-and-Effect Response

Standard

Uses meaning clues to aid comprehension and make predictions about content

Objective

Students practice identifying cause-and-effect relationships in stories.

Materials

- an obvious cause-and-effect story
- Cause-and-Effect Response Sheets, and a large version to display (Appendix C, p. 159)
- Ways to Buddy Read anchor chart (Lesson 27, p. 100)
- chart paper
- markers
- teacher's conferring notebook

Planning

Choose a children's book to read aloud that contains an obvious cause-and-effect situation and pictures that reinforce it.

Procedure

1. **Crafting:** Read a story with several cause-and-effect relationships and think aloud how you identify them.

2. Show students how to look for clue words (e.g., *so, because, since*). Write or draw a cause in the first box of the displayed Cause-and-Effect Response Sheet. Show students how to look for effects by finding other clue words. Write or draw an effect in the second box of the Cause-and-Effect Response Sheet. Have students write or draw the cause and the effect on their own sheets, as well.

3. **Composing:** Have students read independently for 12–15 minutes. Confer with students about causes and effects. Prepare students to teach during the Reflection Session about how they found causes and effects in their reading.

4. Transition to buddy reading for 5–7 minutes. Refer to the Ways to Buddy Read anchor chart. Confer with students.

5. **Reflection:** Ask a few students to share (or have them use turn-and-talk) the cause-and-effect relationships they found.

Points to Ponder

Show students how with each rereading of a book, they gain new insights and understanding.

Replace Tool Kit Materials

Standards

Exhibits care for personal belongings and school materials

Follows classroom rules and routines

Objective

Students learn how to replace their reading tools.

Materials

- sample student Tool Kit (mini Reading Rubric, bookmark, sticky notes, Highlighter Cards)
- replacement tools

Planning

Make a Tool Kit replacement area in your room. Decide how you want to schedule tool replacement: weekly, monthly, on a specific day, or as needed. Create a labeled basket or drawer to organize replacement tools.

Procedure

1. **Crafting:** Tell students that every so often their Tool Kit will need to be refilled. Introduce tool replacement procedures and show students where replacement tools will be kept so students can take responsibility for keeping up their own Tool Kits.

2. In the beginning, younger students may need more guidance or monitoring in this area with gradual release of responsibility as they understand the expectations.

3. **Composing:** Have students practice adding a bookmark or more sticky notes to their Tool Kits from the replacement center.

4. **Reflection:** Brainstorm times that would be appropriate to replace the tools in their Tool Kits.

Points to Ponder

Stock up on sticky notes or ask for parent donations. Photograph the contents of the replacement supplies drawer or basket and display the picture on the front to remind students what is inside and how the supplies are organized.

Look for Cause-and-Effect Relationships

Standard

Knows setting, main characters, main events, sequence, narrator, and problems in stories

Objective

Students identify cause and effect in a story.

Materials

- an obvious cause-and-effect story
- chart paper
- markers
- teacher's conferring notebook
- Book Boxes

Planning

Choose a favorite children's book to read aloud that contains several cause-and-effect relationships.

Procedure

1. **Crafting:** Think aloud as you read the story about the causes you find and the clue words that helped you.

2. Create a T-chart by drawing two columns on a sheet of chart paper. Label one column *Cause* and the other column *Effect*. As you read aloud, record students' thinking about causes and effects.

3. **Composing:** Tell students to continue to look for cause-and-effect relationships in their own reading as they read independently for 12–15 minutes.

4. Confer with individual students about the cause-and-effect relationships they find in their stories. Record your observations. Transition into buddy reading for 5–7 minutes.

5. **Reflection:** Ask students to share cause-and-effect relationships they read or heard. Ask what clue words helped identify these relationships.

Points to Ponder

Depending on your students' level of understanding, continue to revisit cause-and-effect relationships throughout the year and in different genres and content areas so students can transfer this understanding.

Planning Calendar

Lesson 36	Lesson 37	Lesson 38
Introduce Metacognition with a Song Introduce the term *metacognition* and its definition, and teach "The Metacognition Song"	**Use Metacognition to Understand the Characters** Reinforce the use of metacognition	**Use Metacognition to Understand a Story** Understand how being metacognitive helps them better understand a story
Materials chart paper; familiar text; The Metacognition Song poster; Book Boxes; student Tool Kits	**Materials** "The Metacognition Song" poster; familiar book; Book Boxes; teacher's conferring notebook	**Materials** text; Book Boxes; teacher's conferring notebook
Book selections: **Notes:**	**Book selections:** **Notes:**	**Book selections:** **Notes:**

Planning Calendar

Lesson 39	Lesson 40	Reflection
Thinking Strategy: Visualize Introduce visualizing as a thinking strategy	**Thinking Strategy: Activate Schema** Activate schema to help students connect information in a story to their own lives	**What went well?** _____ _____ _____ _____ _____ _____ _____ _____
Materials The Metacognition Song poster; descriptive text; chart paper; Book Boxes; teacher's conferring notebook	**Materials** story to read aloud; Book Boxes; teacher's conferring notebook	_____ _____ _____ **Areas for improvement:** _____ _____ _____
Book selections:	**Book selections:**	_____ _____ _____ _____
Notes:	**Notes:**	_____ _____ _____ _____

Introduce Metacognition with a Song

Standards

Asks questions to obtain information

Uses mental images based on pictures and print to aid in comprehension of text

Relates stories to personal experience

Objective

Teacher introduces the term *metacognition* and its definition and teaches "The Metacognition Song."

Materials

- chart paper
- familiar text
- The Metacognition Song poster (Appendix B, p. 143)
- Book Boxes
- student Tool Kits

Planning

Use a book that allows you to model using several strategies, such as visualizing, predicting, questioning, making connections, and so on.

Procedure

1. **Crafting:** Write *metacognition* on the chart paper. Decode the word and practice saying it together.

2. Tell students that *meta* means "thinking," *cognition* means "your thinking." So, *metacognition* means "thinking about your thinking." Draw a picture to help students visualize its meaning.

3. Teach "The Metacognition Song" (use the tune of "I've Been Working on the Railroad"). Think aloud as you read: "I am picturing…"; "I wonder…."

4. **Composing:** Have students use sticky notes to mark where they stopped to think as they read for 12–15 minutes in their Reading Zones. Transition to buddy reading for 8–10 minutes, and have students show you where they marked their thinking.

5. **Reflection:** Ask students to share how they were able to pay attention to their metacognitive voices. Have them share why thinking about thinking is important.

Points to Ponder

Students are just becoming aware that while they are reading, they are also thinking. Model using all the comprehension strategies, but do not label them. Practice on your own with a challenging adult text and note the strategies and techniques you use.

Use Metacognition to Understand Characters

Standards

Uses mental images based on pictures and print to aid in comprehension

Relates new information to prior knowledge and experiences

Objective

Teacher reinforces the use of metacognition.

Materials

- The Metacognition Song poster (Appendix B, p. 143)
- familiar book with clear pictures of character
- Book Boxes
- teacher's conferring notebook

Planning

Use a text that contains explicit pictures of the main character displaying obvious emotions. Try a new genre or a wordless book.

Procedure

1. **Crafting:** Review the meaning of *metacognition*. Sing The Metacognition Song.

2. Read and think aloud using pictures to understand how the characters are feeling. Ask students to infer what the character is saying, thinking, or feeling. This develops character empathy. Have students turn-and-talk during various points as you read.

3. **Composing:** Confer with students during the entire time. Have students read quietly for 12–15 minutes. Transition to buddy reading and have them share with each other what the characters are saying, thinking, or feeling.

4. **Reflection:** Ask students to share something they have learned during the conferring time about understanding characters.

Points to Ponder

Students may not always have a text that lends itself to the reading goal. If this is an issue, you can always use the story from the think-aloud to confer with students during independent reading. This is called conferring with a book at your side.

Use Metacognition to Understand a Story

Standards

Asks questions to obtain information

Uses mental images based on pictures and print to aid in comprehension

Relates new information to prior knowledge and experience

Objective

Students understand how being metacognitive helps them better understand a story.

Materials

- story to read aloud
- Thinking Strategies poster (Appendix B, p. 144)
- teacher's conferring notebook

Planning

Choose a story that allows the use of several of the thinking strategies (e.g., activating schema, monitoring for meaning, evoking images for visualizing, and making predictions) to introduce these strategies. Display the Thinking Strategies poster.

Procedure

1. **Crafting:** Read a story aloud. Talk about the thinking strategies you use to understand the story.

2. Share your metacognitive thinking: "Something like that happened to me…"; "I understand this character…"; "I picture…"; "I predict…."

3. Ask students to share their metacognitive thinking using turn-and-talk at various times throughout the story. Have students go to their Reading Zones.

4. **Composing:** Have students listen to their metacognitive voices as they read for 12–15 minutes. Have students buddy read and share their thinking for 8–10 minutes.

5. **Reflection:** Confer with students during reading and ask how their metacognitive voices helped them better understand the story.

Points to Ponder

When students turn-and-talk, ask them to share what their partners had to say. This requires them to be better listeners as their partner talks.

Thinking Strategy: Visualize

Standards

Relates stories to personal experiences

Asks questions to obtain information

Uses mental images based on pictures and print to aid in comprehension of text

Objective

Teacher introduces visualizing as a thinking strategy.

Materials

- The Metacognition Song poster (Lesson 36, p. 122)
- descriptive text with cover illustrations
- chart paper
- Book Boxes
- Reader's Notebooks

Planning

Make reduced-sized copies of The Metacognition Song poster to give to students. This lesson will help introduce the thinking strategy of visualizing. Include the sketch used when the song was introduced. Visualizing includes activating the senses through rich detail.

Procedure

1. **Crafting:** Review and sing "The Metacognition Song." Discuss the mental images created by the song. Tell students that visualizing is an important way to understand what you read. Validate their thinking and be sure they give evidence.

2. **Composing:** Have students work in small groups to create illustrations that represent the mental images they visualized from the song.

3. Confer with students as they work. Have students share the mental images they drew.

4. **Reflection:** Students share their own metacognition posters. Have them add their posters to their Reader's Notebooks.

Points to Ponder

Have students work with partners to play guessing games that require one student to describe an object to another student while his or her eyes are closed. This provides practice using descriptive language and visualizing images.

Thinking Strategy: Activate Schema

Standards

Relates stories to personal experiences

Relates new information to prior knowledge and experiences

Objective

Teacher helps students activate their schema to connect information in a story to their own lives

Materials

- story to read aloud
- Book Boxes
- teacher's conferring notebook

Planning

Choose a story with situations that are relatable to the students in your class.

Procedure

1. **Crafting:** Model how to activate your schema by thinking about what you already know about the book you chose just by looking at the cover. Share what you know about the book you selected.

2. Share your thinking with explicit examples: "This reminded me of…"; "This made me think of another story where…." Point out the evidence you used from the text.

3. **Composing:** Have students choose books from their Book Boxes and read quietly for 12–15 minutes.

4. Confer with students as they read. As them to point out their connections to the stories.

5. **Reflection:** Ask students to share the connections they made during independent reading. Compare students' connections and ask how other students' experiences may be changing their own thinking.

Points to Ponder

Have students buddy read and share their connections. When students work together and talk about their connections, they often stimulate each other's thinking.

Notes

Planning Calendar

Lesson 41	Lesson 42	Lesson 43
Thinking Strategy: Predict/Infer Introduce predicting as a thinking strategy	**Thinking Strategy: Monitor for Meaning** Introduce monitoring for meaning as a thinking strategy	**Thinking Strategy: Ask Questions** Use text features to ask questions about the story
Materials illustrated story; Book Boxes; sticky notes	**Materials** fiction or nonfiction text; chart paper; markers; Book Boxes; sticky notes; teacher's conferring notebook	**Materials** fiction or nonfiction text; sticky notes; Book Boxes; teacher's conferring notebook
Book selections: **Notes:**	**Book selections:** **Notes:**	**Book selections:** **Notes:**

Planning Calendar

Lesson 44	Lesson 45	Reflection
Thinking Strategy: Determine Importance Introduce a strategy that helps students determine importance	**Thinking Strategy: Synthesize** Show how to synthesize and summarize information	**What went well?** _____ _____ _____ _____ _____ _____ _____ _____ _____ _____ _____
Materials pictures or items that relate to an outing	**Materials** familiar text (large format); chart paper; markers; sticky notes; Book Boxes; teacher's conferring notebook	**Areas for improvement:** _____ _____ _____
Book selections:	**Book selections:**	_____ _____ _____
Notes:	**Notes:**	_____ _____ _____ _____

Thinking Strategy: Predict/Infer

Standards

Asks questions to obtain information

Uses mental images based on pictures and print to aid in comprehension

Uses meaning clues to aid comprehension and make predictions about content

Objective

Teacher introduces predicting as a thinking strategy.

Materials

- The Metacognition Song poster (Appendix B, p. 143)
- illustrated story

Planning

Inferring begins by making predictions. Choose a story that allows students to use pictures to make predictions, such as *Officer Buckle and Gloria* by Peggy Rathman (1995).

Procedure

1. **Crafting:** Read aloud and point out clues in the illustrations that help predict what will happen. Talk about the thinking strategy you are using.

2. Share what your metacognitive voice is telling you with explicit examples: "I predict…"; "It could be that…"; "This could mean…." Point out evidence in the text that helps you predict.

3. **Composing:** Have students read independently from their Book Boxes for 10–12 minutes. Ask them to use sticky notes to mark a prediction.

4. Confer with students as they read. Ask them to point out evidence that helped them make their predictions.

5. **Reflection:** Have several students share the predictions they made.

Points to Ponder

Starting with predictions allows you to scaffold the learning and to later introduce inference. "Inferences may occur in the form of conclusions, predictions, or new ideas" (Keene and Zimmerman 1997; 2007).

Thinking Strategy: Monitor for Meaning

Standard

Uses self-correction strategies

Objective

Teacher introduces monitoring for meaning as a thinking strategy.

Materials

- fiction or nonfiction text
- chart paper
- markers
- Book Boxes
- sticky notes
- teacher's conferring notebook

Planning

Choose a book that contains unfamiliar or unique words. Explain to students that it is the reader's responsibility to make sure that he or she understands what is being read. Readers must be aware of any confusion and have strategies to help themselves.

Procedure

1. **Crafting:** Read aloud and stop when you come to a difficult word in the text.

2. Label a sheet of chart paper *Monitor for Meaning*. Have students turn-and-talk and tell partners what to do when they come to a word they do not know. Add their ideas to the chart.

3. Have students read independently from their Book Boxes for 12–15 minutes. Ask them to use sticky notes to mark where they did not understand a word. Transition to buddy reading for 8–10 minutes.

4. **Composing:** Confer with students about the places they marked. Ask them to point out their connections.

5. **Reflect:** Have students share the confusing words they found.

Points to Ponder

Thinking strategies can be used to help construct meaning or clarify misunderstandings. Students need to be aware of how to use the strategies for these purposes.

Thinking Strategy: Ask Questions

Standards

Relates stories to personal experiences

Relates new information to prior knowledge and experiences

Objective

Teacher helps students use text features to ask questions about the story.

Materials

- fiction or nonfiction text
- sticky notes
- Book Boxes
- teacher's conferring notebook

Planning

Choose a text that has some confusing or ambiguous information so that students will be able to ask questions before, during, and after reading the text. Model asking questions before you read. Focus on the title, author, and cover illustrations.

Procedure

1. **Crafting:** Write questions that you have about the story on sticky notes and place them on the cover before you start reading.

2. Read the story and stop when you want to ask a question or when you become confused. Write your questions on sticky notes and place them on the text.

3. Share your thinking: "I wonder what it means when it says…"; "I don't understand why…."

4. **Composing:** Have students read independently from their Book Boxes for 12–15 minutes and use sticky notes to mark where they had a question. Confer with students as they read.

5. **Reflect:** Have students share questions they had in their reading.

Points to Ponder

"Asking comprehension questions following reading has limited value in helping teachers learn about children's understanding or in developing children's ability to comprehend" (Fountas and Pinnell 1996).

Thinking Strategy: Determine Importance

Standard

Understands the main idea and supporting details of simple expository information

Objective

Teacher introduces students to a strategy that helps them determine importance

Materials

- pictures or items that relate to an outing, such as camping

Planning

Collect items or pictures to display. Be sure to include pictures of items that are unnecessary, as well, so students can understand how different elements serve different purposes and that some are more important than others.

Procedure

1. **Crafting:** Explain to students that you are planning a trip. List or show all the items you have gathered for the trip, but tell students you are unable to bring everything.

2. Ask students to help you decide which items are the most important to bring.

3. **Composing:** Have students work in small groups to discuss which items they feel are most essential and which could be left behind. Confer with students during their discussions.

4. Have groups share with the class which items they determined were most important.

5. **Reflection:** Ask students why it is necessary to decide that some items are more important than others, and to share the reasons for their choices.

Points to Ponder

Since the purpose of nonfiction reading is often to learn, this strategy will be key to helping students distinguish important from nonessential information.

Thinking Strategy: Synthesize

Standard

Uses visual and verbal clues, including pictures, to comprehend new words and stories

Objective

Teacher shows students how to synthesize and summarize information.

Materials

- familiar text (in a large format)
- sticky notes
- chart paper
- markers
- Book Boxes
- teacher's conferring notebook

Planning

Summarizing is part of synthesizing. It includes identifying key points, such as character, setting, problem and solution, and big idea. Synthesizing is usually done after reading a story. It can evolve as you read and lead to a new understanding of what has been read.

Procedure

1. **Crafting:** Explain that you will be creating a summary for a book you have read. On a sheet of chart paper, write down the story elements from a familiar story.

2. Read aloud. Stop to record different story elements on the chart, including characters, settings, and key plot points. Share your thinking with explicit examples: "This seems like the most important part."

3. **Composing:** Have students read independently from their Book Boxes for 12–15 minutes and use sticky notes to mark important information. Transition to buddy reading. Confer with students about parts of a summary.

4. **Reflection:** Have several students share story elements that they found. Ask students how that information works together to create a big idea.

Points to Ponder

Students can practice summarizing by contributing to a book-review bulletin board or blog. Have them add an illustration to show the main idea of the book.

#50702 –Introducing Reader's Workshop: Preparing Our Youngest Readers

Kindergarten Room

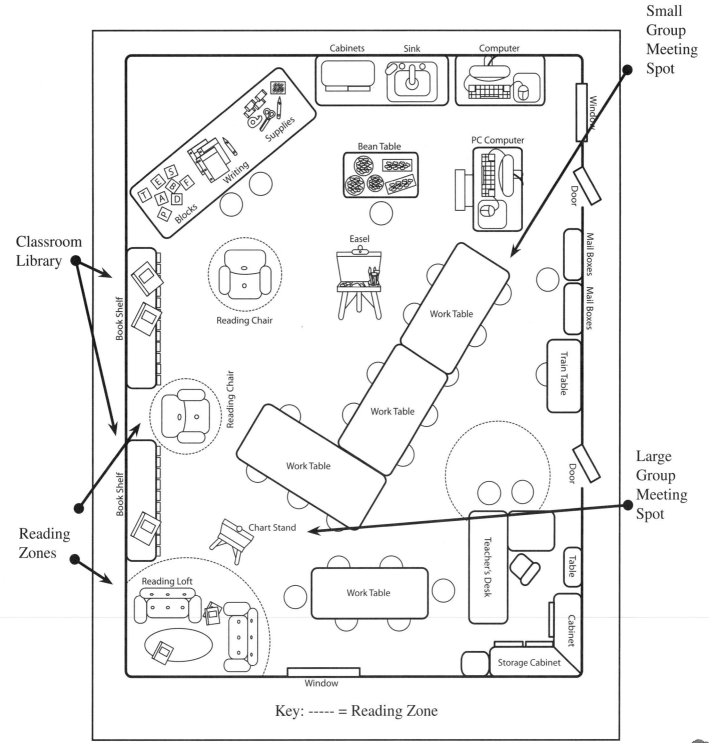

Key: ----- = Reading Zone

Reader's Notebook Title Pages

Directions to the teacher: Use either a composition notebook (kindergarten) or a three-ring binder (first and second grade). Cut apart titles and copy onto card stock for durability, using different colors to help designate sections (e.g., Strategy Work—orange, Reading Reflections—blue).

For kindergarten, cut out and glue the _____'s Reader's Notebook title on the front of the composition book and glue the Strategy Work title to the first page. In the center of the book at the stitched seam, glue the Reading Reflections title on the right-hand side. For first or second grade, copy the _____'s Reader's Notebook onto card stock to use as the binder cover. Glue the Strategy Work title to the first page, or copy onto card stock and insert the page as the notebook's first divider. Make the Reading Reflections page the next divider. *Note*: For a limited budget, use construction paper instead of card stock.

_____'s Reader's Notebook

Strategy Work

Reading Reflections

Books I Plan to Read

Directions to the teacher: Staple five copies of the Books I Plan to Read page inside the front cover of the composition book like a tablet. *Note*: Make sure to have the smooth part of the staple on the outside. Or, use a hole-punch and insert the pages into the front section of a three-ring binder.

Books I Plan to Read	
Book Title	**I Did It!** ✔ / Date

Books I've Read

Directions to the teacher: Use either a composition notebook (kindergarten) or a three-ring binder (first and second grade).

For kindergarten, staple five copies of the Books I've Read page to the inside back cover of the composition book like a tablet. *Note*: Make sure to have the smooth part of the staple on the outside. Or, use a hole punch and insert the pages into the back section of a notebook.

Books I've Read		
Date	**Book Title**	**Genre Code**

Reading Response Sample Letter

Directions to the teacher: Have students use this form to communicate to you about their reading. Students should include a greeting and write the name of the book and the author. Then students can write at least one or two sentences about what they read. Students can summarize their reading or write about specific strategies. Have them sign their letters before turning them in to you. Remember to reply to students about their reading.

A Note About My Reading…

_____

_____

_____

_____

_____

_____

_____

Reading Response Sample Rubric

Criteria	Points Possible	Score
Includes a greeting and a closing	1	
States book title (in appropriate format and underlined) and author	1	
States strategy used	1	
Gives an example of how the strategy was used	1	
Explains how this strategy helped to understand the story	1	
Total Score:		

#50702 –Introducing Reader's Workshop: Preparing Our Youngest Readers ©*Shell Education*

Reading Reflections

Draw a picture about what you read:

Write a sentence explaining what you read:

_____

_____

_____

_____

_____

Teacher response:

_____

_____

_____

_____

_____

Reading Resources

Directions to the teacher: Cut apart the tabs below and copy onto card stock. Have students insert them into their notebooks by taping or stapling them to divider pages or construction paper. Use the blank tab to create new headings as needed.

How to Choose a Book

Book Genres

Fiction

Nonfiction

Book Basics

The Metacognition Song

(sung to the tune "I've Been Working on The Railroad")

I've been thinking about
my thinking.

Metacognition rules!

I've been thinking about
my thinking,

Because reading is so cool!

Can't you see my thoughts
are growing,

Filling up my head.

Now I'm able to understand

All the things that I just read!

#50702 –Introducing Reader's Workshop: Preparing Our Youngest Readers

Thinking Strategies

Metacognition

Monitor for Meaning

Visualize

Ask Questions

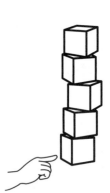

Determine Importance

Synthesize

Activate Schema

Predict/Infer

Conferring Notebook: Layout 1

Directions to the teacher: Use this sheet as you confer with individual students to quickly note a teaching point you offered and a reading goal for that student to achieve.

Thinking Strategy: _____		
Student: **Teaching point:** **Goal:** **Check back:_____**	**Student:** **Teaching point:** **Goal:** **Check back:_____**	**Student:** **Teaching point:** **Goal:** **Check back:_____**
Student: **Teaching point:** **Goal:** **Check back:_____**	**Student:** **Teaching point:** **Goal:** **Check back:_____**	**Student:** **Teaching point:** **Goal:** **Check back:_____**
Student: **Teaching point:** **Goal:** **Check back:_____**	**Student:** **Teaching point:** **Goal:** **Check back:_____**	**Student:** **Teaching point:** **Goal:** **Check back:_____**
Invitational Groups:		

Conferring Notebook: Layout 2

Directions to the teacher: Check off the student's proficiency level in understanding surface structure, and set a reading goal with that student, as well as a date for checking back. Use the suggested sentence starters to evaluate the student's understanding of deep structure. Set a reading goal with that student, as well as a date for checking back. Help students prepare to share their ideas with the class; finally, start organizing your invitational groups.

Student:	Level:

Surface Structure	

	advanced	on-target	needs practice	Reading goal: _____
Decoding	___	___	___	_____
Fluency	___	___	___	_____
Story Elements	___	___	___	Check back: _____

Deep Structure	

Tell me more about…

What did you mean by…?

What are the important ideas?

What is the big idea?

What did you learn about yourself as a reader?

Reading goal: _____

_____

_____

_____

Check back: _____

Preparing for Reflection Session

Tell me what you learned in our conference: _____

How does that help you with your reading? _____

_____

Restate your new learning and tell how it will make you a better reader: _____

_____

Invitational Groups

This student would do well in a group with: _____

_____

Teacher's Tool Kit

Directions to the teacher: Fill a canvas pencil pouch or small plastic baggie with pencils, highlighters, sticky notes, highlighter tape, Highlighter Cards, and bookmarks. For conferring with students, include sight-word cards, a list of thinking stems to start a conference, and Imagery Cards (see pp. 148–150). Imagery Cards help students expand on and add important details as they are visualizing or drawing mental images. Laminate the cards for durability and leave cards with students during a conference as a way to remind them to include more information during their strategy work. Personalize your kit by thinking about other materials you might reference while conferring. Add these to your kit.

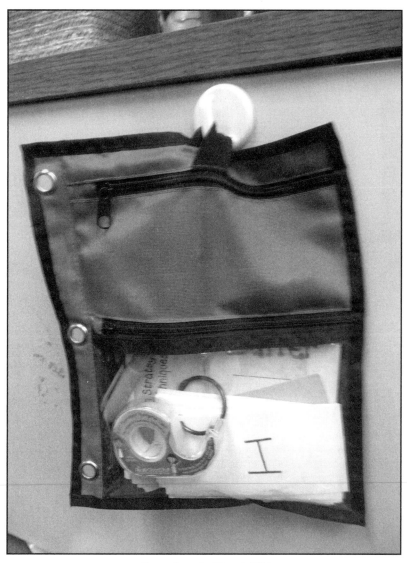

Teacher's Tool Kit

Imagery Cards

Directions to the teacher: Give an Imagery Card to a student during a conference as a reminder of something to pay attention to while reading. (Adapted from *Visualizing and verbalizing: For language comprehension and thinking: Revised edition,* N. Bell, 1986.)

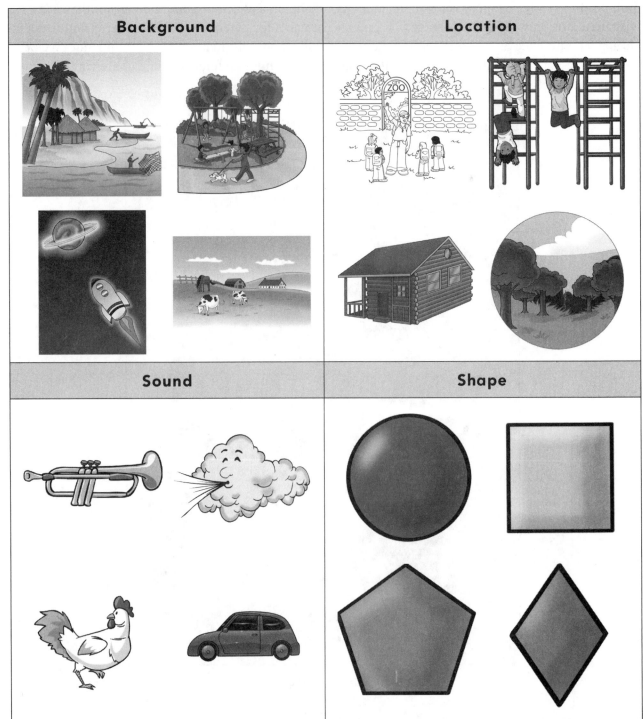

Imagery Cards *(cont.)*

Directions to the teacher: Give an Imagery Card to a student during a conference as a reminder of something to pay attention to while reading. (Adapted from *Visualizing and verbalizing: For language comprehension and thinking: Revised edition,* N. Bell, 1986.)

When	Perspective
Movement	**Mood**

Imagery Cards *(cont.)*

Directions to the teacher: Give an Imagery Card to a student during a conference as a reminder of something to pay attention to while reading. (Adapted from *Visualizing and verbalizing: For language comprehension and thinking: Revised edition,* N. Bell, 1986.)

Nouns	Sizes
person place thing idea	tiny small big giant

Colors	Numbers
	0 5 100 10,000

Sticky Note "Parking Lot"

Directions to the teacher: Circle the icon that corresponds to the strategy used. Fill in the grid with students' names or class numbers. To assess students' use of the strategy of the day, have each student write their initials on a sticky note. As students use the strategies, they place the note on their box on the grid.

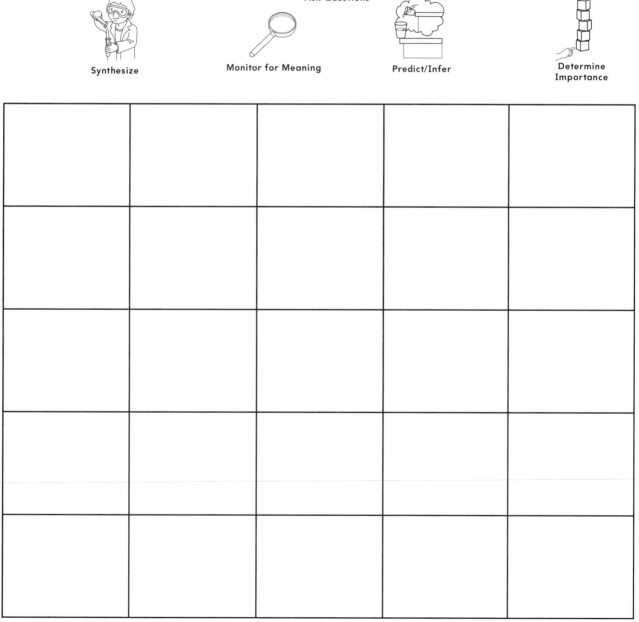

I Can Read...

I can read... **STOP**	I can read..._____.
I can read..._____.	I can read..._____.
I can read..._____.	I can read..._____.
I can read..._____.	I can read..._____.
I can read..._____.	I can read..._____.

Reading Rubric Chart

Super Stars	• read to themselves without bothering others the whole time • stay in their reading spots • take out and read one book at a time • take extra care of their reading books
Shining Stars	• read to themselves without bothering others most of the time • stay in their reading spots • usually take out and read one book at a time • take good care of their reading books
Twinkling Stars	• read some of the time and talk to neighbors • leave their reading spot sometimes • take out several books at a time • are careless with their reading books
Reaching for the Stars	• do not read • leave their reading spots frequently • dump out their books • are careless and destructive with their reading books

Mini Reading Rubrics

Super Stars	• read to themselves without bothering others the whole time • stay in their reading spots • take out and read one book at a time • take extra care of their reading books
Shining Stars	• read to themselves without bothering others most of the time • stay in their reading spot • usually take out and read one book at a time • take good care of their reading books
Twinkling Stars	• read some of the time and talk to neighbors • leave their reading spot sometimes • take out several books at a time • are careless with their reading books
Reaching for the Stars	• do not read • leave their reading spots frequently • dump out their books • are careless and destructive with their reading books

Super Stars	• read to themselves without bothering others the whole time • stay in their reading spots • take out and read one book at a time • take extra care of their reading books
Shining Stars	• read to themselves without bothering others most of the time • stay in their reading spot • usually take out and read one book at a time • take good care of their reading books
Twinkling Stars	• read some of the time and talk to neighbors • leave their reading spot sometimes • take out several books at a time • are careless with their reading books
Reaching for the Stars	• do not read • leave their reading spots frequently • dump out their books • are careless and destructive with their reading books

Super Stars	• read to themselves without bothering others the whole time • stay in their reading spots • take out and read one book at a time • take extra care of their reading books
Shining Stars	• read to themselves without bothering others most of the time • stay in their reading spot • usually take out and read one book at a time • take good care of their reading books
Twinkling Stars	• read some of the time and talk to neighbors • leave their reading spot sometimes • take out several books at a time • are careless with their reading books
Reaching for the Stars	• do not read • leave their reading spots frequently • dump out their books • are careless and destructive with their reading books

Super Stars	• read to themselves without bothering others the whole time • stay in their reading spots • take out and read one book at a time • take extra care of their reading books
Shining Stars	• read to themselves without bothering others most of the time • stay in their reading spot • usually take out and read one book at a time • take good care of their reading books
Twinkling Stars	• read some of the time and talk to neighbors • leave their reading spot sometimes • take out several books at a time • are careless with their reading books
Reaching for the Stars	• do not read • leave their reading spots frequently • dump out their books • are careless and destructive with their reading books

Character and Setting Response Sheets

Directions to the teacher: Display each setting and have students think of characters that they might expect to find in these settings. (Characters do not have to be human!) This will allow the students to associate the characters with the setting of a story. Have them tell why the character fits in that setting. For more practice, cut out and laminate the cards and keep them at a center.

Setting: _____

Characters: _____

_____

_____

Setting: _____

Characters: _____

_____

_____

Character and Setting Response Sheets *(cont.)*

Directions to the teacher: Display each setting and have students think of characters that they might expect to find in these settings. (Characters do not have to be human!) This will allow the students to associate the characters with the setting of a story. Have them tell why the character fits in that setting. For more practice, cut out and laminate the cards and keep them at a center.

Setting: _____

Characters: _____

_____

_____

Setting: _____

Characters: _____

_____

_____

Character and Setting Response Sheets *(cont.)*

Directions to the teacher: Display each setting and have students think of characters that they might expect to find in these settings. (Characters do not have to be human!) This will allow the students to associate the characters with the setting of a story. Have them tell why the character fits in that setting. For more practice, cut out and laminate the cards and keep them at a center.

Setting: _____

Characters: _____

_____

_____

Setting: _____

Characters: _____

_____

_____

Character and Setting Response Sheets *(cont.)*

Directions to the teacher: Display each setting and have students think of characters that they might expect to find in these settings. (Characters do not have to be human!) This will allow the students to associate the characters with the setting of a story. Have them tell why the character fits in that setting. For more practice, cut out and laminate the cards and keep them at a center.

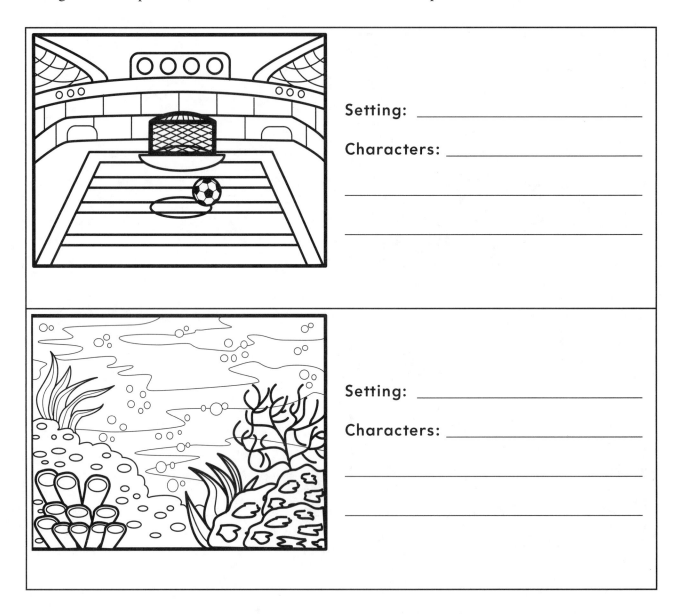

Setting: _____

Characters: _____

_____

_____

Setting: _____

Characters: _____

_____

_____

Cause-and-Effect Response Sheet

Write a sentence or draw a picture to show a cause that occurs in your reading. Write a sentence or draw a picture in the second box that shows the effect of that cause.

If . . .

_____

_____

Then . . .

_____

_____

Reading Resource Tools: Number Words

Directions to the teacher: Copy, laminate, and cut apart on bold lines. Reward students with these reference cards that will help them in their writing. Challenge students to look for these sight words when they read and to use these words in their reflections.

one	1	one	1
two	2	two	2
three	3	three	3
four	4	four	4
five	5	five	5
six	6	six	6
seven	7	seven	7
eight	8	eight	8
nine	9	nine	9
ten	10	ten	10
eleven	11	eleven	11
twelve	12	twelve	12

Reading Resource Tools: Family Words

Directions to the teacher: Copy, laminate, and cut apart on bold lines. Reward students with these reference cards that will help them in their writing. Challenge students to look for these sight words when they read and to use these words in their reflections.

mother		mother	
father		father	
sister		sister	
brother		brother	
baby		baby	
children		children	
grandma		grandma	
grandpa		grandpa	
family		family	
fish		fish	
cat		cat	
dog		dog	

Reading Resource Tools: Color Words

Directions to the teacher: Copy and cut apart on bold lines. Have students fill in the color on the crayon, then laminate for durability. Reward students with these reference cards that will help them in their writing. Challenge students to look for these sight words when they read and to use these words in their reflections.

red		red	
yellow		yellow	
pink		pink	
green		green	
purple		purple	
orange		orange	
blue		blue	
black		black	
brown		brown	
white		white	
lavender		lavender	
turquoise		turquoise	

Reading Resource Tools: Contractions

Directions to the teacher: Copy, laminate, and cut apart on bold lines. Reward students with these reference cards that will help them in their writing. Challenge students to look for these words when they read and to use these words in their reflections.

can not	can't	can not	can't
do not	don't	do not	don't
they are	they're	they are	they're
would not	wouldn't	would not	wouldn't
does not	doesn't	does not	doesn't
should not	shouldn't	should not	shouldn't
must not	mustn't	must not	mustn't
is not	isn't	is not	isn't
will not	won't	will not	won't
could not	couldn't	could not	couldn't
it is	it's	it is	it's
we will	we'll	we will	we'll

Setting Picture Cards

Directions to the teacher: Use these cards for setting and character practice. Ask students whom they would expect to find in each setting and why. Laminate and cut apart to use at centers.

Setting Picture Cards *(cont.)*

Directions to the teacher: Use these cards for setting and character practice. Ask students whom they would expect to find in each setting and why. Laminate and cut apart to use at centers.

Bookmarks with Decoding Strategies

Directions to the teacher: Copy the bookmarks onto card stock and have students keep them in their Tool Kits for reference. Fill in the blank bookmark with different strategy tips. Laminate the bookmarks for durability.

Strategies for: Figuring Out Unknown Words

1. Chunk it out.

    ex: /wag/-/on/

2. Look for a smaller word inside the larger word.

    ex: wag/on

3. Look for picture clues.

    When you think you know...

4. Ask yourself: Does it make sense? Does it sound like language?

Strategies for

_____

_____

Highlighter Cards for Tool Kits

Directions to the teacher: Copy onto card stock, laminate, and then cut the cards apart. Place one piece of highlighter tape in each of the four boxes. Have students add the cards to their Tool Kits as an additional resource.

Before returning Book Boxes, have students find and remove highlighter tape from their books and return it to their Highlighter Cards. Make sure they find and return all four pieces.

Highlighter Card	Highlighter Card	Highlighter Card
1.	1.	1.
2.	2.	2.
3.	3.	3.
4.	4.	4.

Cipher Wheel

Directions to the teacher: Write one the names of half of your students inside each wedge of the larger wheel and the names of the other students inside each wedge of the smaller wheel. Enlarge both wheels to poster size if possible, then cut out the wheels and attach them with a brad in the center. Spin the inner wheel so that student names line up. Assign partners according to the alignment of the two wheels.

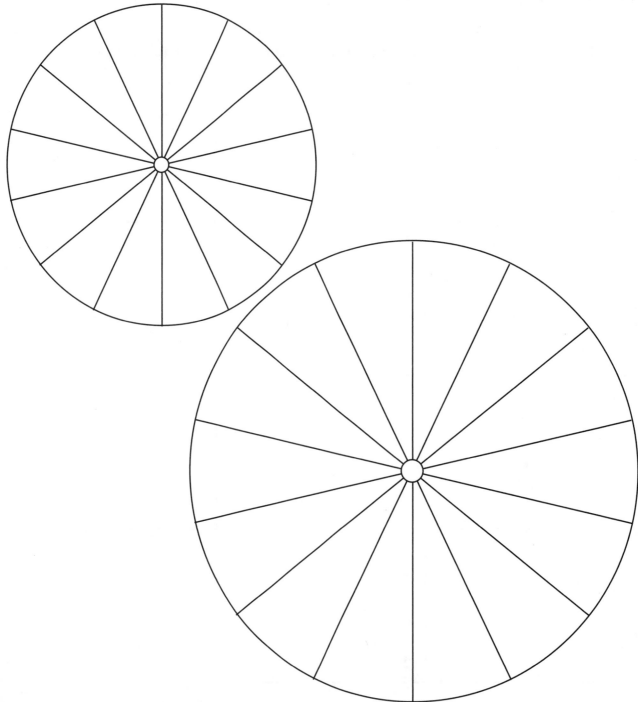

Tick Tock Pals

Directions to the teacher: Give each student a clock face with his or her name written in the middle. On each of the blank lines (3 o'clock, 6 o'clock, 9 o'clock, 12 o'clock) have students set meeting times by writing one student's name at each time. Students must coordinate so that they do not double-book an appointment.

To assign buddies, call out a time and tell students to work with that buddy. Students keep their Tick Tock Pals sheet in the Reader's Notebook to reference. (***Note:*** Also, keep a copy of everyone's clock yourself as a reference.)

Provide guidelines as to how many boys or girls each clock must have. Add lines (up to 12 buddy options), or substitute shapes for the numbers, depending on the needs of your students.

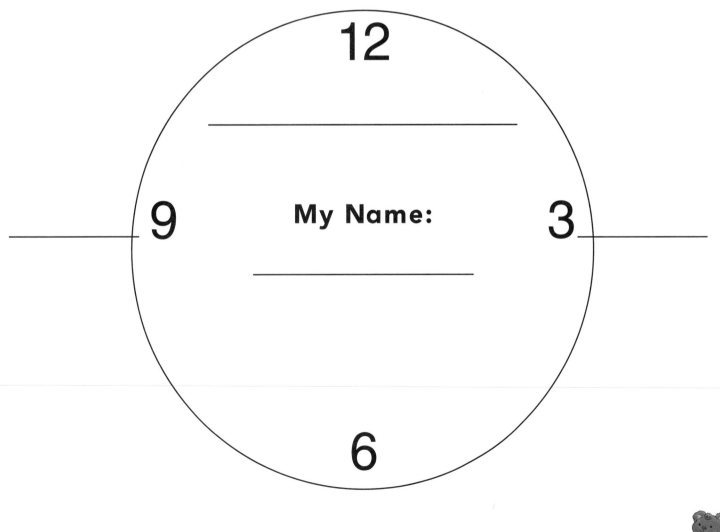

Appointment Buddies

Directions to the teacher: Give each student an appointment sheet. Have students fill in the sheet with the names of their classmates. Students must coordinate so that they do not double-book an appointment. Choose an icon and tell students to work with that buddy. Students check their appointment charts to see whom they have for that appointment. Students keep their charts in the Reader's Notebook to reference. (***Note:*** Keep a copy of all charts for yourself, as well.)

_____'s Appointment Buddies

_____'s Appointment Buddies

_____'s Appointment Buddies

_____'s Appointment Buddies

Cordial Calling

Directions to the teacher: Have students practice appropriate social skills by inviting buddies to read with them. Ask three to five students if they would like to invite a friend to read with them. Students who are invited to be buddies may say "yes," or may choose to read alone. (If a student says "no" to one student, he or she may not choose to read with a different student.)

Make sure to vary the students who are called to choose buddies first so all have turns asking and responding.

Dear _____:

Would you like to read with me?

Please answer

Yes _____ or No _____.

Return to: _____

References Cited

Bell, N. 1986. *Visualizing and verbalizing: For language comprehension and thinking: Revised edition*. San Luis Obispo, CA: Gander Publishing.

Block, C., L. Gambrell, and M. Pressley. 2002. *Improving comprehension instruction: Rethinking, research, theory, and classroom practice*. San Francisco, CA: Jossey-Bass.

Calkins, L. 2001. *The art of teaching reading*. New York, NY: Longman.

Collins, K. 2004. *Growing readers: Units of study in the primary classroom*. Portland, ME: Stenhouse Publishers.

Cunningham, P. M., and R. L. Allington. 1999. *Classrooms that work: They can all read and write*. New York, NY: Longman.

Dorn, L., and C. Soffos. 2005. *Teaching for deep comprehension: A reading workshop approach*. Portland, ME: Stenhouse Publishers.

Fountas, I. C., and G. S. Pinnell. 1996. *Guided rading: Good first teaching for all children*. Portsmouth, NH: Heinemann.

Hindley, J. 1996. *In the company of children*. Portland, ME: Stenhouse Publishers.

Keene, E. 2008. *To understand: New horizons in reading comprehension*. Portsmouth, NH: Heinemann.

Keene, E., and S. Zimmerman. 2007. *Mosaic of thought: The power of comprehension strategy instruction*, 2nd ed. Portsmouth, NH: Heinemann.

Keene, E., and S. Zimmerman. 1997. *Mosaic of thought: Teaching in a readers' workshop*, 1st ed. Portsmouth, NH: Heinemann.

McGregor, T. 2007. *Comprehension connections: Bridges to strategic reading*. Portsmouth, NH: Heinemann.

McNamara, D. S., ed. 2007. *Reading comprehension strategies: Theories, interventions, and technologies*. New York, NY: Lawrence Earlbaum Associates, Inc.

Miller, D. 2002. *Reading with meaning: Teaching comprehension in the primary grades*. Portland, ME: Stenhouse Publishers.

———. 2008. *Teaching with intention: Defining beliefs, aligning practice, taking action, K–5*. Portland, ME: Stenhouse Publishers.

Newingham, B. n.d. *Rockin' room 13*. Detroit, MI: Troy School District. **http://hill.troy.k12.mi.us/ staff/bnewingham/myweb3/.**

Paterson, K. January 1999. Back from IBBY. *The Horn Book Magazine* 75(1): 26.

Pearson, P. D., J. A. Dole, G. G. Duffy, and L. R. Roehler. 1992. Developing expertise in reading comprehension: What should be taught and how should it be taught? In *What research has to say to the teacher of reading*, 2nd ed., eds. J. Farstup and S. J. Samuels. Newark, NJ: International Reading Association.

Professional Resources

There are many types of professional resources available to assist you with the implementation of Reader's Workshop. Books, conferences, and colleagues are just a few.

Here is a list of the books and websites that inspired us throughout this journey and have continued to help us grow and develop. These would be excellent resources for book study among your grade level or whole school. Be willing to give and receive new ideas and strategies. Help each other extend beyond established comfort zones. Having educational discourse with your learning partners opens many doors to a world of new thinking and ideas—just as it will for your students!

In addition, see the Teacher Resource CD for a list of recommended children's literature that will work well when introducing many of the thinking strategies. Feel free to choose your own selections, as well.

Anderson, Carl. *How's It Going?: A Practical Guide to Conferring with Student Writers.* 10th ed. Portsmouth, NH: Heinemann, 2000.

Boushey, Gail, and Joan Moser. *The Daily Five: Fostering Literacy Independence in the Elementary Grades.* Portland, ME: Stenhouse Publishers, 2006.

Diller, Debbie. *Spaces and Places.* Portland, ME: Stenhouse Publishers, 2008.

Hindley, Joanne. *In the Company of Children.* Portland, ME: Stenhouse Publishers, 1996.

The Kansas Coaching Project. 2009. *Thinking Devices: Engaging Students Through Prompts that they Can't Resist Talking About.*

Keene, Ellin Oliver. *To Understand: New Horizons in Reading Comprehension.* Portsmouth, NH: Heinemann, 2008.

Keene, Ellin Oliver, and Susan Zimmermann. *Mosaic of Thought, Second Edition: The Power of Comprehension Strategy Instruction.* 2nd ed. Portsmouth, NH: Heinemann, 2007.

LikeToRead.com. http://www.liketoread.com/ (Accessed Oct. 2009)

McGregor, Tanny. *Comprehension Connections: Bridges to Strategic Reading.* Portsmouth, NH: Heinemann, 2007.

Miller, Debbie. *Reading with Meaning.* 1st ed. Portland, ME: Stenhouse Publishers, 2002.

Miller, Debbie. *Teaching with Intention.* Portland, ME: Stenhouse Publishers, 2008.

Term Index

anchor chart—Charts created as a class to assist in the building of Reader's Workshop structures or appropriate vocabulary when using the comprehension strategies.

book nook—Specified area in the classroom designed for the specific purpose of reading, often decorated thematically, with specific emphasis on the comfort of the reader.

call-and-response—A way to use polite language to invite a student to share their thinking or instruct the class.

deep comprehension—Those texts that cause the reader to go beyond literal comprehension by combining the text with the reader's own prior knowledge to construct understanding.

deep structure—Text that requires the application of the seven comprehension strategies (schema, mental images, questioning, inferring, determining importance, synthesis, monitoring for meaning), focusing specifically on the understanding of text rather than the reading of text.

demonstration—Instruction or examples of the proper behaviors used during Reader's Workshop.

document camera—A visual presentation tool capable of projecting objects onto a wall or screen, allowing the students to see modeling at a more personal level.

environmental print—Symbols, words, signs, or numbers found in everyday life and recognized in the specific context.

invitational group—Small group of students invited to gather together to work with the teacher on a specific, common need.

lexical system—Internal reading system allowing the student to recall words without decoding.

Meeting Spot—Area designed for whole-group (Large Group Meeting Spot) or small-group (Small Group Meeting Spot) lessons. Often comprised of a large carpet and easel to aid in the crafting and reflection sessions.

metacognition—Thinking about your thinking. The awareness of one's thinking when reading text.

modeling—Teacher demonstration or think-aloud, especially in the application of comprehension strategies.

old favorite—Books that hold special meaning to the reader. These books usually have been read repeatedly throughout childhood and are books that you wanted to read again and again.

piggy-backing—Adding on to another person's thinking in a discussion.

Reading Zones—Spaces around the room for students to read independently or with buddies.

silent signals—Signals a teacher uses to redirect students without stopping the lesson. Often these include hand signals or small gestures.

surface structure—The application of skills used to decode words in the text including the recognition of sight words.

think aloud—Time when a teacher models the thinking processes used to understand a piece of text. The act of vocalizing the thought processes to help students understand the use of the comprehension strategies.

thinking device—Thought-provoking objects teachers use to prompt dialogue between students or between teacher and student.

thinking stems (sentence frames)—Sentence starters to assist students in developing appropriate vocabulary when verbalizing their thinking in a text related to the comprehension strategies.

Contents of Teacher Resource CD

Page	Title	Filename
Planning Calendars		
36–37	Establish Procedures and Book Care	calendar1.pdf
48–49	Introduction to Thoughtful Reading	calendar2.pdf
60-61	Book Choices and Reading Practices	calendar3.pdf
72-73	What Thoughtful Readers Do	calendar4.pdf
84-85	Elements of a Story	calendar5.pdf
96-97	Reading Strategies	calendar6.pdf
108-109	More Reading Strategies	calendar7.pdf
120-121	Thinking About Your Thinking	calendar8.pdf
128-129	Active Reader's Workshop	calendar9.pdf
Appendix A: Sample Floor Plan		
135	Kindergarten Room	floor_plan.pdf
Appendix B: Teacher Resources		
136	Reader's Notebook Title Pages	title_pages.pdf
137	Books I Plan to Read	plan_to_read.pdf
138	Books I've Read	I_have_read.pdf
139	Reading Response Sample Letter	response_letter.pdf
140	Reading Response Sample Rubric	sample_rubric.pdf
141	Reading Reflections	reflections.pdf
142	Reading Resources	resources.pdf
143	The Metacognition Song	metacognition.pdf
144	Thinking Strategies	thinking_strategies.pdf
145	Conferring Notebook: Layout 1	layout1.pdf
146	Conferring Notebook: Layout 2	layout2.pdf
147	Teacher's Tool Kit	tool_kit.pdf
148–150	Imagery Cards	imagery_cards.pdf
151	Sticky Note "Parking Lot"	parking_lot.pdf
152	I Can Read…	I_can_read.pdf
153	Reading Rubric Chart	reading_rubric.pdf
154	Mini Reading Rubrics	mini_rubrics.pdf

Contents of Teacher Resource CD *(cont.)*

Page	Title	Filename
Appendix B: Teacher Resources *(cont.)*		
155–158	Character and Setting Response Sheets	character_setting.pdf
159	Cause-and-Effect Response Sheet	cause_effect.pdf
160–163	Reading Resource Tools: Number Words, Family Words, Color Words, and Contractions	resource_tools.pdf
164–165	Setting Picture Cards	setting_cards.pdf
173	Recommended Reading	recommendedreading.pdf
Appendix C: Student Resources		
166	Bookmarks with Decoding Strategies	bookmarks.pdf
167	Highlighter Cards for Tool Kits	highlighter_cards.pdf
Appendix D: Buddy Reading Management Systems		
168	Cipher Wheel	cipher_wheel.pdf
169	Tick Tock Pals	tick_tock_pals.pdf
170	Appointment Buddies	appointment_buddies.pdf
171	Cordial Calling	cordial_calling.pdf